77 impactful
projects

Ideas for a
Better World

GOOD By DESIGN

First published and distributed by
viction:workshop ltd.

viction:ary™

viction:workshop ltd.
Unit C, 7/F, Seabright Plaza,
9-23 Shell Street,
North Point, Hong Kong
Url: www.victionary.com
Email: we@victionary.com

 @victionworkshop
 @victionworkshop
Bē @victionary
 @victionary

Edited and produced by viction:ary
Creative direction by Victor Cheung
Book design by viction:workshop ltd.
©2022 viction:workshop ltd.

ISBN 978-988-79727-7-8
Printed and bound in China

77 impactful
projects

Ideas for a
Better World

GOOD By DESIGN

PREFACE

Design has always played a big role in shaping civilisation. From graphics, media and means of communication to products, fashion and interiors, it has enhanced, enriched and empowered humanity in a variety of ways. Beyond its aesthetic factor, good design serves as a powerful force that can shift perspectives and behaviours, influencing how we think, feel and do. By conceptualising and executing novel strategies, ideas and innovations, designers can wield their skills and abilities to raise awareness, call for action and manifest change on a global scale.

In the last two years, the COVID-19 pandemic has truly upended life as we knew it. As we slowly come to grips with a new reality, countless uncertainties still loom in the horizon. However, one thing has become clearer than ever: the urgent need for us to not only rethink the way we care for our planet and well-being as a whole, but to actually take immediate and present action for the not-too-distant future. Although our challenges seem insurmountable today, the responsibility falls on each and every one of us to do something — anything — right, because every little step counts towards building a brighter tomorrow for humankind.

As the outbreak continues to force many industries like the health, safety and wellness sectors to reexamine their processes and outputs — pushing more businesses to prioritise digital transformation and sustainability to survive — its implications are striking an even deeper chord with the visionaries, movers and shakers who simply want to do good. Whether it is to introduce different schools of thought and habits or to plug existing gaps in society, these change-makers, who come in all sorts of sizes, shapes and forms, are going forth fearlessly to help us navigate the post-pandemic landscape and protect everything we love for as long as possible.

Designers are having to respond and adapt to our new ways of living and working in faster and more flexible ways, while preparing for the road ahead. Besides the studios making a positive impact through their portfolio in this book, IDEO (ideo.org), The Good Tribe (thegoodtribe.com) and Design to Divest (design-todivest.com) are among the growing number of entities committed to meaningful projects that rewire our brains and repair our communities by drawing on creativity, collaboration and values like fairness, inclusivity and accountability.

Underlined by passion, their efforts are further boosted by corporations that are finally listening to what their investors and customers are saying to drive sustainable operations. More and more big brands like Lego and Adidas are releasing environmentally friendly lines for the discerning, while Environmental, Social, and Governance (ESG) funds and social venture capitalist firms are on the rise worldwide. Completing the ecosystem are non-governmental and non-profit organisations like 350 (350.org), Change.org (change.org) and Food Tank (foodtank.com) that focus on educational causes and campaigns to turn ripples into waves and tides of transformation.

Although the pace has picked up recently, there is still a long way to go on our collective journey forward. In the course of publishing this book, we have learned that even though change may seem impossible at times, it is important to never give up. 'Good by Design' salutes all the heroes who are doing good with their design skills, striving to make our world a better place, and giving us hope amid the gloom — one creative step at a time.

SPECIAL
FEATURE

① Eisuke Tachikawa @ NOSIGNER
② Simon Caspersen @ SPACE10
③ Eddy Yu & Hung Lam @ CoDesign Ltd
④ Jason Little @ For The People

NOSIGNER

Dialogue with Founder
Eisuke Tachikawa

When it comes to ideas, Japan is brimming with exciting ones. Drawing on their rich history and heritage, its artisans, creatives and innovators are able to fuse the old and the new to deliver high quality craftsmanship with a distinctly Japanese flavour. Amid its vibrant creative landscape, NOSIGNER sets out to drive social change today towards more hopeful tomorrows. Using design as a tool, it looks at the best connections and relationships in the elements around us, in searching for clues that carry the potential for change. Underlining the studio's work is its founder Eisuke Tachikawa's unique philosophy known as 'Evolution Thinking', a method that draws on the evolution of living things who have constantly created over time to generate new ideas and foster game-changers. In the following Q&A, Tachikawa shares more about his creative explorations and solutions for humanity's future.

TOKYO BISHOKU

Together with the creative team responsible for producing the 'Tokyo Bousai' disaster preparation book and Chef Masahiro Kasahara from 'Sanpiryouron' in Tokyo, the NOSIGNER team developed three meals in pursuit of deliciousness. To complement the food, they created a concept book with the view that magazine-style designs would likely be delivered regularly in the future like a subscription to solve problems such as inaccessibility to food warehouses during emergencies.

How did your design career begin? What is a day in your studio like?

Up until graduate school, I studied architectural design under Kengo Kuma. Perhaps I was overthinking it, but during that time, I was not sure where architecture began and where it ended.

I was constantly asking questions like, is furniture part of a building's architecture? Are the signs on the walls architecture? Through these questions, I came to develop an interest in other disciplines of design. I then began studying industrial and graphic design on my own and started designing as NOSIGNER in 2006 to pursue design in a broader sense.

When I first started, I worked anonymously; somewhat like Banksy. However, after five years, the Great East Japan Earthquake, which caused the greatest economic damage from an earthquake in human history, prompted me to move on from anonymity so I could work on the OLIVE project. Since then, NOSIGNER has become a design consultancy that works on social design.

We are a select few, and I am still deeply involved in every project, primarily in conceptualisation and design. NOSIGNER is located in Yokohama's Chinatown, and as I also live there, I can spend time with both my family and my colleagues whether I am working from home or in the office. It is a beautiful neighbourhood with the seaside and parks nearby. I spend about half the day on meetings with clients or lectures and my free time on communication with my team and writing activities. A harmonious balance between work and life is ideal to me, so my current working style suits me.

What is your definition of 'design for good'?

It is important to create beautiful relationships with the future of a project and its environment in mind. Beautiful relationships are just as important as a beautiful form. By prioritising both, relationships and form can create a harmonious balance. This naturally enhances the form, making it even more beautiful.

What inspired you to focus your design skills for good?

We create social design because we do not want to design without meaning. When you pursue meaningful design seriously, you will naturally arrive at projects that are beneficial to society. Therefore, it is also important for our clients to be partners in aspiring to a greater meaning.

SOCIAL HARMONY

As part of PANDAID's activities, the team at NOSIGNER developed a signage system that played musical notes whenever people stepped on the musical score on the floor. Set to 'Gymnopédie n°1' by Eric Satie, each note on the score triggers a different sound effect, so that the order in which the notes are played would change with the person's steps, as the rhythm changed with their pace. By making the most of the power of classical music, culture, and art, NOSIGNER aimed to subliminate the act of social distancing by making it into a rich way of communication.

"WHY and HOW to make something are far more important questions than WHAT to make."

What do you hope to achieve through your projects?

I want to create hope in industrial settings, nurture more creative people, or preserve culture and the ecosystem to pass on to future generations. In order to do so, we undertake appealing design projects (social design), study and teach the essence of creativity from the perspective of biological evolution ('Evolution Thinking'), and propose policies and visions for these aims.

How has designing for good improved your skills as a designer, and changed you as a human being?

WHY and HOW to make something are far more important questions than WHAT to make. WHY and HOW are two parts of a set. Leaning too far in either direction weakens the project. To pursue designs beneficial to society, one needs to look at the WHY, with design skills being the HOW. Working on projects beneficial to society may not necessarily improve your design skills. However, when you possess highly developed design skills and are working on designs beneficial to society, you have the power to change the world.

In many cases, projects which address a major WHY cannot be accomplished by designers alone. In other words, the bigger the objective, the more design naturally tends toward collective intelligence. In such cases, designers require skills as an administrator who sets forth a vision and as a facilitator who builds a consensus among diverse people. While it may be unusual to call this 'design', creating projects with a beautiful form is what I believe design is all about.

How do you think designers can change the world through their work? What values, skills, or experiences would they need to have?

Being a designer is a wonderful job through which you make things concrete. It is wonderful because the world can only change through the transformation of concrete things. However, I am not sure if most designers are aware of the impact of changing the concrete. Although making the smallest changes to what we usually create could change our impact on the environment or our relationship with society, without an awareness of this, creative changes may be quite difficult to achieve.

A few years ago, I began advocating an approach called 'Evolution Thinking', which studies the true nature of creativity from the perspective of biological evolution, and recently wrote a book about it. It is a bestseller in Japan. Biological evolution occurs through a cycle of mutation and adaptation. To put this in terms of creativity, these are, in other words, the ability to change the current situation and the ability to understand relationships. There are different ways of practicing each of these two things. If it has been published in your country, please give it a read by all means.

TOKYO BOUSAI

How/why did you decide to work on the brief?

The Great East Japan Earthquake that occurred on March 11, 2011, not only caused tremendous damage to the Tohoku region, the epicentre of the quake, but also had a huge impact on Tokyo, which is located 370 km to the southwest, causing difficulties to many wanting to return home. With a 70% probability of an earthquake occurring directly beneath the Tokyo metropolitan area within the next 30 years, it is easy to imagine that the Tokyo-Yokohama area, with its large concentration of people, would be severely damaged. In fact, the Comprehensive Natural Disaster Risk Index has reported that Tokyo is the city with the highest disaster risk in the world. However, until now, disaster prevention-related information provided by the government and other organisations has not been able to reach many Tokyo residents due to its lack of appeal and realism. Under these circumstances, we have been working to change Tokyo from the city with the highest risk of disaster in the world to the city with the best disaster preparation.

What were your key considerations overall when it came to working on this project?

For this project, I was very mindful about making it entertaining. By making full use of various expressive methods such as characters, cartoons, illustrations, infographics, etc., and taking universal design into consideration, we created content that could entertain all generations and, at the same time, remind them of the reality of disasters and raise their awareness of disaster prevention.

What was your creative starting point for this project? Where did you find your inspiration from?

Up until a year before this project, I served for half a year as the concept director of the Japanese Cabinet's Cool Japan policy. During that time, I put together and presented a proposal stating that we should be able to use content industries like manga and anime to solve societal problems, but the Cabinet was restructured soon after, and that proposal wasn't really put to effective use — which was extremely regrettable. I wanted to prove that the power of design and content industries can be used for impactful policies. That became the main motivation behind this project.

What were the challenges you had to overcome in the course of completing this project?

Decision making for government-issued designs is complicated, so undertaking a project such as this is accompanied by a lot of hardships. Despite consulting with the government while making our proposal, bidding competitions for the project were opened numerous times. The government's decision-making process became the biggest hurdle.

How do you hope this project will influence viewers?

TOKYO BOUSAI was one of the largest publishing projects in the history of the Japanese government, and as a result, information about the book spread on social networking sites every time a major disaster occurred in various parts of Japan, fundamentally overturning the nature and image of disaster prevention in Japan. Most Japanese people are now aware of TOKYO BOUSAI.

After TOKYO BOUSAI, many similar designs using yellow and black as key colours have been seen, changing the image of disaster prevention in Japan. We believe that it is a one-of-a-kind project that has proven that the power of design can contribute to saving as many lives as possible. As disasters continue to happen around the world, I want people to feel that design is by no means powerless under these circumstances, and that we can create a more resilient society by changing people's thinking.

TOKYO BOUSAI

NOSIGNER designed and edited the disaster preparation book 'Tokyo Bousai', which was distributed to all households in Tokyo in collaboration with DENTSU advertising agency. Since 2015, it has reached over 6.6 million people, out of the 8.03 million copies printed. As a universal design, the team used key 'warning colours', namely yellow and black, so that the book could be located easily, complemented by manga drawings that clearly illustrated methods to protect oneself from disasters. The team were also cognisant about appeal, making content easy to understand through eye-catching drawings to be understood — even by those with no clue about disaster preparation.

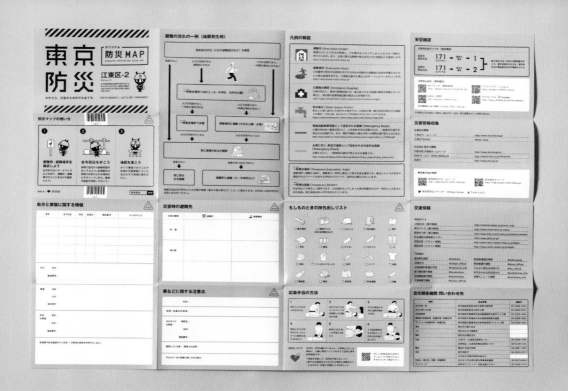

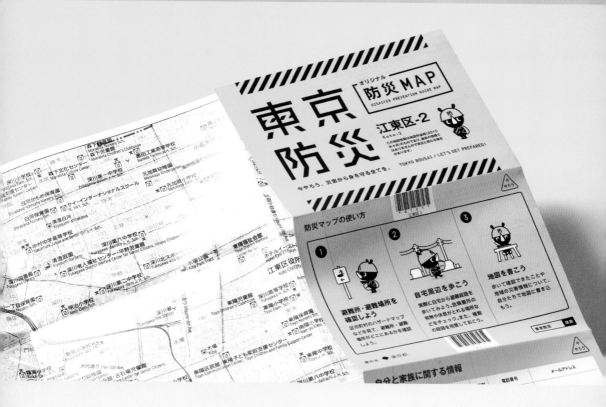

OLIVE

As a result of searching on the Internet for several hours after the occurrence of the Great East Japan Earthquake, the team at NOSIGNER realised that there were tons of people who wanted to help the affected areas as much as they did. Although people were sharing information about the disaster online, as it was a colossal disaster, the speed of information being uploaded was too rapid and disparate — making it hard for people to keep track of all the details. This necessitated a place to store and organise all the useful information collated, which is why OLIVE was created as a helpful wiki site.

OLIVE

How/why did you decide to work on the brief?

At 14:46 on March 11, 2011, the Great East Japan Earthquake occurred, hitting a staggering M9.0. Besides the catastrophic damage it caused along the East coast of Japan, with a death toll of 18,434 people and 25,000 others reported missing, the resulting tsunami destroyed the Fukushima nuclear power plant stations. The earthquake has since gone down in world history as the biggest disaster of the last 100 years. Under such circumstances, we knew we had to do something to help restore the lifelines that had been cut off so abruptly. Although there was almost nothing we could do through design, we believed that this was the time when the possibilities of human creativity could shine.

OLIVE is a wiki site that gathers and shares practical knowledge during a disaster, created just 40 hours after the Great East Japan Earthquake. Derived from NOSIGNER's wish for Japan to 'Live On', the name combines the letter 'O' (an emblem of the Japanese national flag) and 'LIVE'. Through help from all corners of the world, ideas were quickly gathered on how to build what was necessary to survive in affected areas that were not getting supplies in time. OLIVE achieved over one million page views within three weeks, where information was estimated to have been delivered to at least 10 million people, thanks to the Ministry of Health and Welfare, television stations, newspapers, and other platforms. OLIVE has been translated by volunteers into English, Chinese, and Korean, and is still expanding today as a database of disaster countermeasures using collective intelligence.

What were your key considerations overall when it came to working on this project?

To help areas affected by the disaster as quickly as possible, we went ahead with a project which prioritised openness over quality to allow anyone to participate. I believe the result of this emphasis on speed and connections was ultimately positive. Although the final contents might have been rough in some ways, it was proof of how easy participation was. As a result, about 200 volunteers came together, and made significant achievements as a disaster prevention campaign involving people from all across Japan.

What was your creative starting point for this project? Where did you find your inspiration from?

Even before the earthquake, we were promoting open-source design projects and sharing intellectual property which aimed to help people improve their creativity and convey the value and joy of creating something with your own hands. It is precisely because we had this running start that we were able to launch this project immediately.

What were the challenges you had to overcome in the course of completing this project?

As the problems resulting from the earthquake were far greater than the challenges of the project itself, we worked with a single-minded intensity to create something that might be of some use. While I think our abilities were limited, the human spirit and ability to go on living is incredible, so within about half a year, things more or less returned to normal in the areas affected by the disaster.

How do you hope this project will influence viewers?

I want people to feel that actions and projects close to them can give rise to major projects that involve society at large. I believe that appeals and plans elucidated through design can help to move the uninvolved and apathetic.

PANDAID

How/why did you decide to work on the brief?

On April 5, 2020, as the world teetered on the brink of declaring a state of emergency, NOSIGNER launched PANDAID, a collaborative website that collects wisdom from around the world to help people change their lives and habits to protect themselves from a pandemic. COVID-19 is a serious infection that can be severe and even deadly at times. However, many infected people are asymptomatic, and the main characteristic of the disease is that it can spread without people even realising it. The fear of this invisible infection has already driven some countries into a corner, but actions can be taken to minimise its spread. We knew that it was the time to make the most of our creativity and design knowledge to heal the pain in our world.

What were your key considerations overall when it came to working on this project?

Our editorial emphasis goes towards providing scientific facts in ways that are easy to understand and implement. Underlined by this direction, the PANDAID book collates a variety of facts and tips on everything from the basics of infectious diseases to prevention methods, including how to stay strong and work remotely. In addition, we design infographics and posters as needed to deliver intuitive content that the public can easily understand.

We also devote our efforts into design that can be immediately useful to healthcare providers. For example, we developed a face shield that can be made in seconds from an A4-sized clear plastic page. It is extremely cheap and practical, and the sheet design can be downloaded for free. The instructional video for making the face shield received more than 1 million views on social media and YouTube, and it was also covered on TV and other media. This garnered many responses, with Kitasato University Hospital producing 10,000 of its own face shields at the hospital, along with many others like Tokyo University Hospital. Groups ranging from major corporations to primary school children have also made their own face shields. Yahoo! JAPAN mass-produced 8,000 at their corporate offices, while others made cases of donations to healthcare providers.

What was your creative starting point for this project? Where did you find your inspiration from?

I live in Yokohama's Chinatown, and Yokohama was the port where the COVID-19-stricken Diamond Princess docked. When this happened, the neighbourhood became deserted, and two of my favourite Chinese restaurants went out of business in rapid succession. I was deeply saddened that my neighbourhood would die out if things went on like this, so I started this project.

What were the challenges you had to overcome in the course of completing this project?

In this project, it goes without saying that the problems facing society were far greater than the challenges of the project. In the end, we may not have been able to defeat COVID-19, but I believe we showed one way of fighting it.

How do you hope this project will influence viewers?

We each possess creativity, and I want people to feel that we can overcome major problems by using our collective strength. We will have to persevere a while longer until we overcome COVID-19. Let's do our best!

PANDAID

In response to the COVID-19 crisis, the team at NOSIGNER launched PANDAID to help people protect themselves and their loved ones from the virus while alleviating anxiety. Before information is published on the PANDAID site, it is vetted by a diverse group of volunteers, including medical professionals, designers and social activists, to ensure that content is based on scientific fact. The information is also presented in a way that is engaging and easy to understand, so that anyone can put the tips into practice.

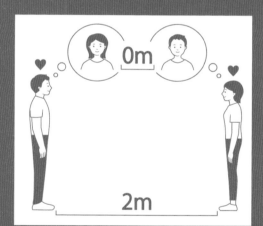

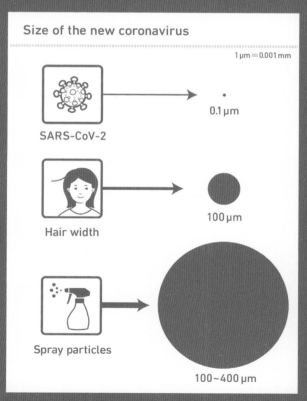

Size of the new coronavirus

1 μm = 0.001 mm

SARS-CoV-2 → 0.1 μm

Hair width → 100 μm

Spray particles → 100~400 μm

PANDAID FACE SHIELD

To raise public safety during the COVID-19 pandemic, the team at NOSIGNER developed a face shield that could be easily made from an A4-size clear file. The face shield takes no more than 30 seconds to complete — and all people have to do is place a printed template onto a clear file and cut along the lines. Since it was introduced, its tutorial video has been viewed more than one million times on social media. Besides generating a lot of attention, the face shield has also been used in various medical facilities.

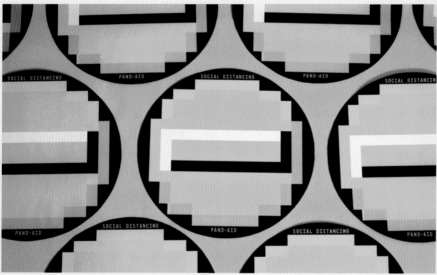

LIFE COIN STICKER

The LIFE COIN STICKER was developed as the PANDAID organisation worked on resuming their economic activities while taking into account pandemic-imposed social distancing. Each floor sticker, which mimicked the shape of coins used in games, also incorporated a motion sensor as a feature, emitting a distinctive sound effect the moment people stepped on it. Typically, coins in games are a symbol and motif for increasing life – a concept that ultimately inspired the NOSIGNER team to create the stickers, in hoping that people would be more cognisant of protecting their lives and loved ones.

SPACE10

Dialogue with Co-founder & Communications Director
Simon Caspersen

Sometimes, the most extraordinary ideas and solutions are
inspired by the most ordinary of objects or circumstances.
Driven by its distinct view of what our future could look
and be like, SPACE10 has been committed to changing
the world through its life-centred design and community-
centric projects, one innovative concept at a time. Set
up as an external and independent research and design
lab, it works exclusively with IKEA to prime the furniture
brand, a global favourite for its stylishly simple Swedish
sensibilities, into a mighty force for change, underlined by
the mission to create a better everyday life for people and
the planet. In the following Q&A, we find out how its diverse
multidisciplinary team, comprising talented individuals
from a variety of fields like aeronautical engineering,
food design, and architecture, tackle various issues like
affordable housing and urban farming around the world.

How did your studio begin?

It all began when Inter IKEA Group CEO Torbjörn Lööf reached out to SPACE10's co-founder Carla Cammilla Hjort, to discuss co-strategising a better future for IKEA. They had gotten acquainted through an earlier collaboration on a limited product series for IKEA. Carla and fellow co-founder Simon Caspersen pitched the idea of setting up an external and self-governing research and design lab to work exclusively for IKEA to explore new ways of fulfilling IKEA's overall vision of creating a better everyday life for the many people.

What SPACE10 brings to IKEA is an outside-in approach to innovation, and another possibility to pursue radical solutions, beyond what might come intuitively to the IKEA organisation of today. We're set up as an external and independent research and design lab, yet we are entirely dedicated to IKEA. We look into new directions and contribute to making IKEA on the forefront and ready for change — which seems to be the only constant in the fast-paced world we live in.

Source: Digital Design Lead Tommy Campbell for DesignWanted

What drives your team?

We value humility and curiosity in the highest sense. Ideas are not proprietary secrets to be hidden behind lock and key so much as they are living, breathing things that need oxygen and discussion to really flourish. We work with a global, creative network of experts and forward-thinking partners who can challenge us on our ideas and improve them via collaboration. We always try to judge our work by how it performs for someone else in their everyday life. A specific style or form factor will always be less important to us than making things that just simply work for people.

Source: Digital Design Lead Tommy Campbell for DesignWanted

What is your definition of 'design for good'?

We tend to design for those who already have a lot of choices, and ask ourselves: Who are we improving life for? Most innovative investments are being put forward for the top 50% of the world who already have a middle and high-income class. I believe, in the future, that successful companies will realise the other 50% as a huge opportunity, and start doing good for people who do not have a lot today. From IKEA's perspective, democratic design is concerned with combining sustainability, form, function and quality — all at a low price.

It means that when you design, you make sure that those designs are available for the many. If not, then it's not democratic design. That would be like a democratic election in which only 20% of the world population could vote, because they had access to the means that could buy them a ballot with their name.

(Source: Managing Director Kaave Pour for Copenhagen Institute for Futures Studies)

What inspired you to focus your capabilities for good?

If you look at the world right now, it's clear that humans and the designs we have made are not going according to plan. We have had a tradition of making something that is relevant for people, and then everything else is a by-product. Now we are lonely. We are polarised. We are f*cking up the planet, to put it mildly, and that's because we only talk about putting people in the centre of design. So I welcome the posthuman design era, where humans are part of the equation — just not at the expense of everything else. This has been called 'people-planet design', 'life-centred design' and 'system-driven design', in which we can only create a good life for people if we create a good life for the planet.

Source: Managing Director Kaave Pour for Copenhagen Institute for Futures Studies

What do you hope to achieve through your projects?

We focus on three major shifts that inform all our work:

- Societal shifts: The societal changes in the coming decade are complex — from political and economic uncertainty; to a global housing crisis; to an increasing lack of critical resources like food, energy and clean water and people rising up demanding a more fair and equal society to live in.
- Environmental shifts: We are in the middle of a climate emergency and it is accelerating faster than most scientists anticipated. The next ten years will be the most critical decade in human history.
- Technological shifts: The pace of technological change is increasing exponentially, which both presents new ethical questions while making us far better equipped to take on the challenges we face.

In my eyes, the biggest creative challenge we face as designers today, is how we transform our current consumption-oriented economic system into a self-sustaining society — one that is more equal, dignified, happy and human.

Source: Digital Design Lead Tommy Campbell for DesignWanted

How do you think designers can change the world through their work? What values, skills, or experiences would they need to have?

I hope more responsibility accompanies the possibility of solving problems and making solutions. It is not going to fly if, in today's world and with so much inequality, you are fortunate enough to be working with design, and take that opportunity for granted by benefiting only yourself and your peers. In the future, there will be so many structural challenges that if you're not part of the solution, you will be part of the problem. Designers are already escaping companies that are not purpose- or value-driven.

Keep bringing optimism back into dystopian and pessimistic discussions, because if we don't believe the future can be better and nobody tries to make it better, then we've already lost. And I hope you have learned to be more patient already. It's not just about where you're going, but also about how you feel while you are going there. Being happy, being excited about what you do and living your values along the way is as important as the goal itself.

Source: Managing Director Kaave Pour for Copenhagen Institute for Futures Studies

EVERYDAY EXPERIMENTS

Through the Everyday Experiments project, SPACE10 set out to find out how tomorrow's technologies could redefine the way we live at home. To help imagine new ways of living, the team developed a collection of digital experiments with some of the most innovative design and technology studios around the world that shared the same curiosity for the latest innovative breakthroughs and an interest in having fun with them as well. The result is an array of clever ideas, radical proposals and exciting prototypes that each challenge the role of technology in the home — taking the everyday and making it extraordinary.

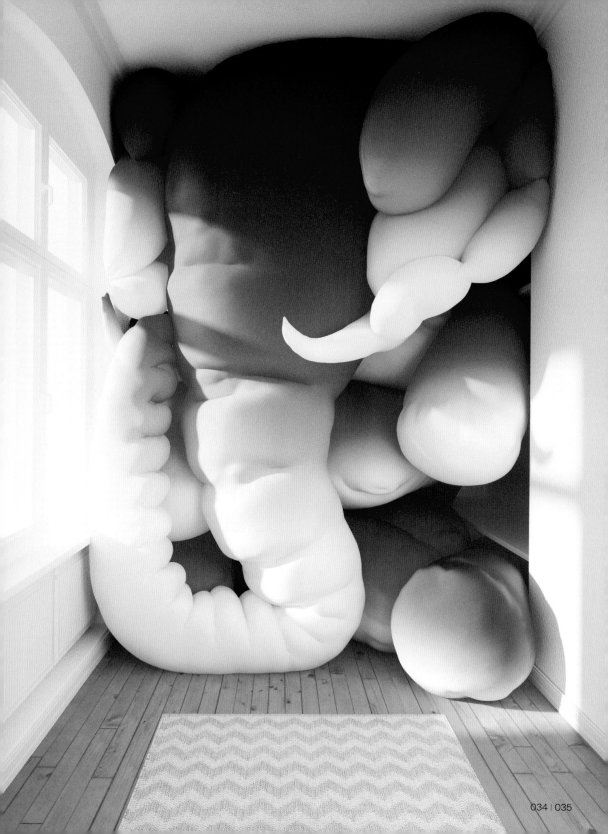

"In the future, there will be so many structural challenges that if you're not a part of the solution, you'll be a part of the problem."

Everyday Experiments

How/why did you decide to work on the brief?

With people spending more time at home than ever before, now is the time to act and learn more about the way we experience and engage with our homes. Throughout this past year, technology played its most integral role in keeping us connected to our families, our work, our hobbies. At times, we felt enabled by technology. Other times, it felt hard to escape. At IKEA, home should always be about people first. By letting technology into our homes, we wanted to explore how it can be part of our everyday lives, while making sure we still feel safe and free in our spaces. It is integral to us at IKEA that as we continue to stay better connected with people through technology, that we place high value on privacy and preserving the boundaries between public and private.

What were your key considerations overall when it came to working on this project?

Tranquility is of the utmost importance when designing technological features for the home. One's home should be the point that people look to having the most peaceful interactions; a place of comfort and serenity. Technology shouldn't distract from that peace, but rather act as an enabler to almost make us believe that our homes just know us.

What was your creative starting point for this project? Where did you find your inspiration from?

When we think of 'home', technology is not necessarily the first thing that comes to mind. IKEA and SPACE10's Everyday Experiments is a way of exploring how simple, beautiful, friendly digital creations can improve aspects of everyday home life — to take our preconceptions that technology can be intrusive, untrustworthy or confusing, and prove that it can actually be peaceful, helpful, secure and sustainable.

To help us imagine new ways of living, we called upon the minds of some of the most innovative design and technology studios in different corners of the world. They put their heads together and started creating proposals to add to an ongoing series of digital experiments.

How do you hope this project will influence viewers?

Technology in the home doesn't only have to mean doing something faster, or with more precision. It can simply provide a way to enjoy our homes more: infusing the spaces we have with joyous elements that make you feel happy, calm, or safe.

The experiments applied the latest technology available today to experience-driven details of everyday living. Taking relatively mundane aspects of day-to-day life, such as opening the blinds, choosing a lamp, rearranging the furniture or looking for a new couch, they worked to discover how these could be made easier, quicker, more enjoyable or more sustainable. They also explored avenues that weren't just functional, but fun: turning your space into a musical instrument, or seeing how furniture would look and behave if it was a friendly creature.

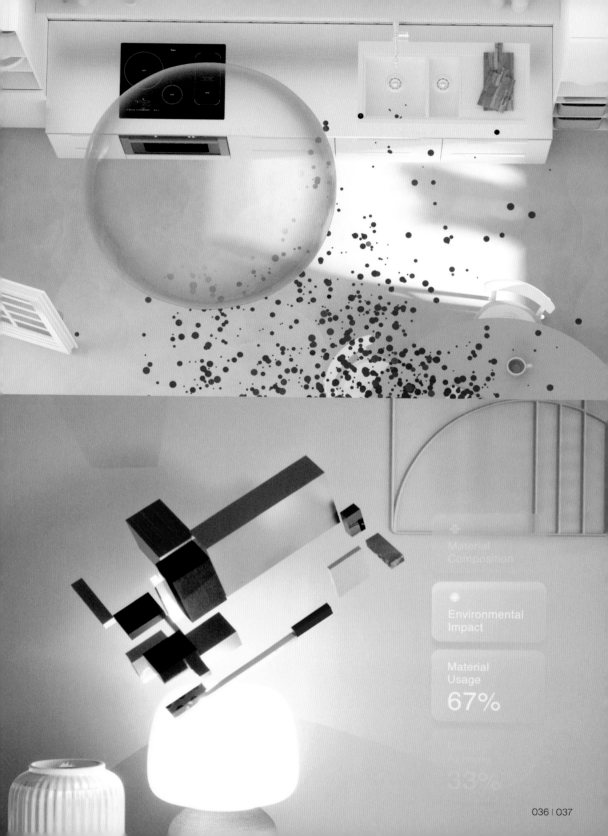

Material
Composition

Environmental
Impact

Material
Usage
67%

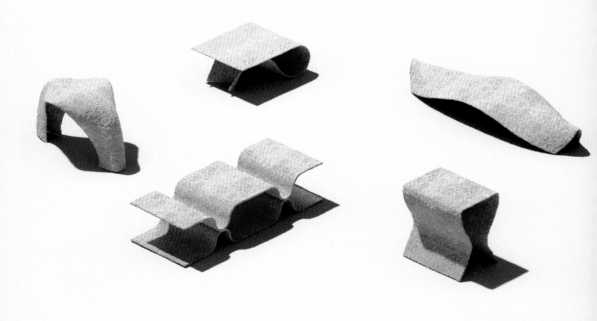

BIO-FOLD

Through Bio-Fold, architects Katya Bryskina and Tomás Clavijo sought to explore questions like 'how can we develop more sustainable furniture fabrication using existing everyday objects?' during their residency at SPACE10, as part of its collaboration with Strelka Institute. They combined their expertise and shared passion for sustainability to turn biocomposite 'waste' into viable materials for fabricating furniture.

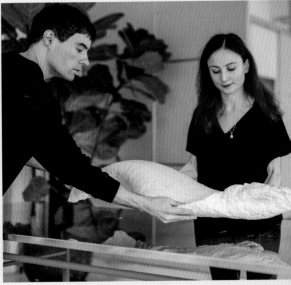

Bio-Fold

How/why did you decide to work on the brief?

From laundry and storage to gardening and transportation, few IKEA products have as many creative uses as the FRAKTA shopping bag, which is why it was the perfect place to start experimenting with circular fabrication methods using everyday tools, biodegradable materials, and a touch of imagination.

What was your creative starting point for this project? Where did you find your inspiration from?

Agricultural production disposes of great amounts of waste, in the form of vegetal fibres. On a global scale, these natural by-products show significant promise for the production of biodegradable composite materials, or simply biocomposites. Biocomposites are formed by mixing vegetal fibres with a natural binder — such as plant-based resin or bicarbonates — and compressing the material into a solid form. As a material, they are renewable, cheap, biodegradable and in many cases completely recyclable.

When communities are empowered with the right methods and tools, vegetal fibres can turn from 'waste' into 'material' — and become a cheap and locally sourced material for the production of everyday objects.

Katya and Tomás experimented with biodegradable binders and vegetal fibres to create materials that could be used for fabricating furniture. However, the perfect recipe for biocomposite furniture production is yet to be discovered. Therefore, we've decided to share our exploration with the world to take further.

How do you hope this project will influence viewers?

Using simple household tools and the ubiquitous FRAKTA bag means that this process could be used by anyone, anywhere, to create circular furniture from their own home. This opens up the opportunity to encourage truly democratic expansion of circular design.

To provide instructions for how to create furniture out of biocomposites, Katya and Tomás designed a step-by-step guide, using the FRAKTA shopping bag and everyday tools likely to be found in a regular home.

Unlike traditional IKEA assembly instructions, this guide doesn't come with neat pre-prepared toolkits. The first thing to do is to make sure you have access to the necessary equipment and materials. The next step is to transform FRAKTA into a sealable object that can be used as a cast. To do this we've outlined 12 steps for how to cut, fold, and glue the two bags, from start to finish. Finally, you're ready to start the creation process. Simply follow the 7 steps for mixing the vegetal fibres and binders in FRAKTA, deflate the bag, shape your design, and let the biocomposites dry. The curing time depends on the binder, so before you remove the cast, make sure your furniture is completely solid. The furniture produced in this way is made out of completely biodegradable material. To dispose of the furniture, simply treat it as you would with any other organic waste — head to your nearest biowaste station, or let it decompose in nature.

Ultimately, Bio-Fold is not a recipe for transforming linear production into circular. Rather, we wish to highlight the opportunity for how everyday objects and materials — with a bit of imagination — can enable sustainable fabrication, use, and recycling of products.

The Urban Village Project

How/why did you decide to work on the brief?

Cities all around the world are facing rapid urbanisation, ageing populations, climate change and a lack of natural resources. At the same time, we are in the middle of a global housing crisis. Our cities are becoming increasingly unaffordable, unsustainable and socially unequal — and the situation is only becoming more challenging. 1.5 million people are moving to a city every week, meaning that in just a little over a decade, 1.6 billion people are projected to lack access to affordable, adequate and secure housing.

On top of this, we face another challenge: people are living closer and are more connected than ever before, but we still feel increasingly lonely, anxious and stressed.

It's in the intersection of these pressing challenges where SPACE10 and EFFEKT Architects believe The Urban Village Project might offer a solution. We know that around 40% of the areas that need to be urbanised in 2050 do not yet exist, meaning that as daunting as the task is, we have a blank canvas to explore how we want the future of our cities to look like and function.

What were your key considerations overall when it came to working on this project?

Liveability: The Urban Village Project is a vision for creating shared living communities for people of all ages, backgrounds, and living situations. The objective is to enable a better everyday life through the multiple benefits of living in a tight-knit community, with shared facilities and services, like daycare, urban farming, communal dining, fitness, and shared transportation. These benefits not only offer a sense of belonging: they're proven to boost health and happiness too.

Sustainability: The Urban Village Project sets out to make sustainable living a seamless part of daily life through integrated solutions like water harvesting, clean energy production, recycling, local food production and localised composting. Even the whole architectural framework is rooted in sustainable materials and a circular approach to our built environment.

Affordability: The standardised modular building system of The Urban Village Project can be pre-fabricated, mass-produced and flat-packed — all of which would help drive construction costs down. But just as importantly, The Urban Village Project challenges existing models of development, and seeks to finance the construction through partners who look for long term investments. Combining this with democratic setups inspired by community land trusts and co-operatives, The Urban Village Project could secure the interests of the community and allow cheaper homes to enter the market.

How do you hope this project will change urban living in the future?

The Urban Village Project would enable more people to become homeowners by creating a form of housing co-operative. With significantly lower monthly rents and more disposable income, this unique legal setup would allow residents to buy 'shares' in the property — when they want to and when they can. This would get rid of expensive down payments upfront alongside interest rates which limit first time buyers from entering the housing market. Over time, the property would be owned by the community, and residents would be able to sell their shares back to the cooperative.

THE URBAN VILLAGE PROJECT

The Urban Village Project by SPACE10 and EFFEKT Architects rethinks how we design, build, finance and share our future homes, neighbourhoods and cities. Besides envisioning cross-generational shared facilities where private and community spaces are interspersed harmoniously, the project also proposes offering multiple apartment types and making sustainability a seamless part of daily through integrated solutions like water harvesting, renewable energy, local food production and localised composting.

THE GROWROOM

The Growroom by SPACE10 was designed in collaboration with architects Sine Lindholm and Mads-Ulrik Husum as an open-source, spherical garden that enables people to grow food locally and sustainably. An urban farm pavillion and a prime example of what food-producing architecture could be like in the future, as well as how it could help humanity, the Growroom was created to trigger conversations about how to meet the rising demand of food in growing cities. Local versions of the Growroom have since been built across the world as far afield as Helsinki, Moscow, Rio de Janeiro, San Francisco, Seoul and Sydney.

SOLARVILLE

SolarVille was a Playful Research project that set out to reimagine our energy system in the pursuit of democratising access to clean energy, materialising as a working prototype of a miniature neighbourhood completely powered by solar energy. Built to a 1:50 scale, some households could generate their own renewable energy through solar panels, while others automatically purchase excess electricity directly from the producer using blockchain technology.

SolarVille

How/why did you decide to work on the brief?

Around 2 billion people in the world still have little to no access to electricity, with 860 million people living with absolutely no access at all. It's an almost impossibly expensive task to reach these people with the centralised energy networks we have in place today, often because they're too slow and economically adequate to reach those locked in energy poverty. SolarVille aims to showcase that, when combined, technologies such as solar panels, micro-grids and blockchain open new opportunities for off-grid systems — allowing people to leapfrog traditional grid electricity.

What were your key considerations overall when it came to working on this project?

If solar power is cheaper than any other source of new power in most parts of the world, then why isn't all of our electricity coming from solar?

- Huge amounts of coal and gas-generating capacity are already installed. These power plants will continue to produce energy as long as they make just enough money for their managers to keep the doors open.
- In many countries, total electricity demand is falling and it is more difficult to invest in solar if power needs are met by existing plants.
- Storage is still expensive. Without storage, solar is both intermittent and, in many places, unreliable. In order to ensure around-the-clock electricity, you have to factor in the cost of a storage device, which might double the cost of night-time power in a sunny country.

Despite the obstacles referred to above, solar's future is bright. Solar energy is not a fuel that can be used up, but a technology that is constantly being developed. Because of that, we can expect a continuous fall in prices associated with relying on solar energy for our electricity needs. Ultimately, that will make clean energy cheaper and more accessible into the indefinite future.

SPECIAL FEATURE — SPACE10

LOKAL

LOKAL was born in the heart of Shoreditch during the week-long London Design Fair. It was the name for the tasty salad bar and farm that was set up on the sidelines of SPACE10's pop-up to give visitors the chance to see a hydrophonic system up close. Featuring technology like vertically-stacked trays containing nutrient-enriched water, LED lights and computerised automation, LOKAL attracted curious passers-by and diners who tucked into the nutritious greens prepared by chef Simon Perez. creating conversations around the new ways with which we can produce more food with less, in a more sustainable way than we do today.

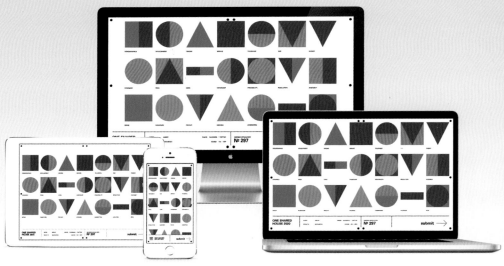

ONE SHARED HOUSE 2030

Launched in collaboration with Anton & Irene, a design practice based in New York, One Shared House 2030 was designed as an online application form for a hypothetical co-living space opening in 2030. The questions that were asked in the form revolved around the goods and services potential applicants would be willing to share, such as kitchens, workspaces, childcare, and self-driving cars, as well as what kind of co-living space would ultimately suit them. Through the project, SPACE10 hoped to gain an insight into what ideal co-living spaces would look like in the future, as shared living grows in popularity.

CoDesign Ltd

Dialogue with Co-founders
Eddy Yu & Hung Lam

No human is an island, which is why the best ideas are often created by people, for people, with people. Without tapping onto a shared set of beliefs and collaborative action, change can seem impossible — which is why CoDesign studio, and its award-winning sister platform CoLAB, is all about coming together to use the power of creativity for good. Co-founders Eddy Yu & Hung Lam were colleagues early on in their design careers before finding themselves working side-by-side again after embarking on their own personal journeys, evolving as a team to specialise in projects beyond visual branding, publications, packaging and promotions to push for social innovation through design. Through CoLAB, they hope to synergise the forces of commercial, cultural and social entities to consciously set betterment in motion — sharing more about some of their best projects in the following Q&A.

GREEN@COMMUNITY RECYCLING STORES

The Community Recycling Network rebranding scheme was an initiative by the Environment Protection Department to promote recycling in Hong Kong, China. This initiative also included the launch of recycling stores across 18 districts in the city. In envisioning a unified and ubiquitous network of recycling hotspots, CoDesign was driven by the concept of creating friendly and trustworthy neighbourhoods, designing 'convenience stores' of recycling that combined a bold and sleek image with a professional experience.

How did the studio begin?

Eddy: We met when we were designers and ex-colleagues at Kan & Lau Design Consultants in Hong Kong, China. In 2003, I set up CoDesign before getting Hung to help out. Eventually, he began taking on a more comprehensive role in branding and packaging design and working on bigger projects, kickstarting the partnership. We ran as a two-man band for about half a year before adding more staff, focusing on commercial and cultural projects at first before taking on more branding projects four to five years later. During these years, we both really began to understand the power of branding. Better branding can lead businesses to a lot of rewards, especially in terms of money.

Hung: CoLAB, short for 'collaboration' and 'laboratory', was founded in 2010 as a way to check ourselves. We hoped to discover what design could be used for — the true meaning and power of design. The financial crisis in 2008 and its impact on the world's economy made us feel like 'accomplices' in 'selling lies' in a way, especially if we continued not representing brands truthfully or working for brands we did not trust or believe in ourselves. The economic downturn gave us more free time to reexamine our motives and switch our focus to something new, where we could explore other possibilities.

Eddy: Our first social project was for Cafe 330 by the New Life Psychiatric Rehabilitation Association. They had a very low budget and we had to strike the right balance between their commercial earnings from the eatery and their social mission to help others. Throughout the process, we kept asking ourselves if design could truly make a difference for a good cause, and it was quite a struggle at that point.

Hung: It was also difficult to find a good balance because of the conflict: improving the cafe's branding would result in more earnings and customers, or better business as a whole, but it would also place more stress upon the staff, who were people recovering from mental illness. So what's the bottom line here? It's always the question.

What is your definition of 'design for good'?

Hung: It's not about the social cause. I think designing for good is the very original purpose of design — but the purity of its meaning has been tainted by the modern world. Agendas have been added to reach goals/targets and turn design into something different, and we should always check that. It's like a pyramid — at the 'top', most designers work for 'wealthier' clients for more profits, while at the 'bottom', the designers tend to think that they are getting fewer 'rewards'. However, it's not always the case. I think we should strive towards being in the 'bottom' sector.

Eddy: Design is a solution for daily life and asks questions towards a better, easier life. However, mass production, industrialisation and commercialisation have resulted in many unnecessary products being produced at cheap costs. Many parties also make use of design as an excuse to gain the biggest market share. Everything with the word 'design' in it is seen to gain more profits and this is how design is being distorted in the modern world. Therefore, we should rethink the purpose of design and if we are really in need of these products. It is wrong to only calculate direct production costs without considering indirect costs like fair wages, benefits for workers, and environmental impact. The lack of awareness of all of the above has caused us to produce more waste and problems for our world, which is why 'design for good' should be more about getting a better balance and returning to the pure origins of design.

"I think designing for good is the very original purpose of design — but the purity of its meaning has been tainted by the modern world."

What inspired you to focus your design skills for good?

We like to explore new sectors/areas/relationships and how they can be sustained further. The line has become very blur now and there is almost no pure commercial project in our portfolio today. In fact, more than 70% of our work comprises social projects.

We see the need for social enterprises to learn how to allocate their resources properly, especially for design, and want to help them with their initiatives. The recent pandemic has also given us a chance to reexamine what we've been doing so far and we are thankful to be less affected (compared to studios that mainly work for commercial clients). The most basic human needs still exist during the pandemic and social projects are still going on, so they almost serve as a reward for all our hard work.

What do you hope to achieve through your projects?

We hope that the distorted values of the current commercial operating system can be corrected with the public's attitude becoming more positive, potentially leading to a 'commercial market 2.0' to make businesses with good causes more sustainable.

How has designing for good improved your skills as a designer, and changed you as a human being?

Eddy: Personally, I've gained different perspectives that have changed the way I look at things. In terms of commercial projects, I've learned to find a balance between understanding the clients' needs, meeting customer needs, earning profits, and getting rid of competitors. Through our social projects, I've discovered how important it is to make an impact on people, create behavioural change, inspire action, and speak in front of a bigger crowd that is not just limited to our clients.

When it comes to communication design, I define/consider 'value' differently. Ultimately, communication design is about selling a product/service as well as the value you are concerned about, which means promoting what we actually believe in.

Skills-wise, my design approach has evolved. My commercial work looks less 'fancy' for more visual appeal, vs. the down-to-earth language in my social projects. The latter is more mission-oriented and interactive, underlined by a close relationship to daily life, because of the involvement of many different stakeholders.

What values, skills, or experiences would designers need to have to change the world through their work?

Hung: Empathy — to understand others, the world, and what they need.

Eddy: If a designer does not have a good attitude towards work/life, things get distorted pretty quickly. They would also be more susceptible to stress and wanting to give up. Some designers stay away from social projects because they are not award magnets and do not generate enough buzz to make the designers famous. However, all this really depends on how you view/value work/life.

SO...SOAP!

'So...Soap!' was a community-based organic soap production scheme that aimed to generate job opportunities for underprivileged women in the society. Inspired by its distinctive naming and logo design, which reflects the meanings of 'genuine soap' and 'soap for society', CoDesign sought to highlight the scheme's positive values in an eye-catching way through effective design. The project received positive feedback from different layers of society and walked a journey different from the usual personal care brands.

So...Soap!

How/why did you decide to work on the brief?

Leila Hiu Lui Chan, a friend of ours who is an award-winning author and well-known journalist in Hong Kong (China) introduced us to the client, Bella Ip, as she knew we wanted to work on more social projects.

What were your key considerations overall when it came to working on this project?

Bella is a soap maker who owned a soap brand, Bella Sapone, before approaching us. Back then, her product packaging was relatively raw and rough. She used to work with schools and got to know many other single mothers like herself, who had to make ends meet by working multiple jobs. However, this made it hard for them to spend time with their children, resulting in the latter picking up the wrong values and becoming rebellious.

As her brand began getting more attention/support, she started thinking about improving her branding and making soaps on a bigger scale. At the same time, she was inspired to help the single mothers and pass her skills on to them, so they could earn their living through independent means and do what they really wanted to do. Bella then set up a community centre that provided family-friendly jobs, but money was always the first and biggest constraint.

We had just set up CoLAB around then — and the timing couldn't have been more perfect for us to work together, so we suggested rebranding and promoting the brand as an investor, and if the brand succeeded, we would then start product- and profit-sharing in return.

What was your creative starting point for this project?

Bella is an environmentalist and makes biodegradable soap with 100% natural ingredients. She found a soya milk brand using an environmentally friendly material for their bottles and came up with the idea of collecting and recycling their used bottles for her soaps and other products in liquid form. On the packaging, we featured the districts where each bottle of soap was produced through numbers and initials. For example, '1/TP' meant that the soap was produced in the project's first production district, Tai Po.

What were the challenges you had to overcome?

The project lasted for 10 years and we had several challenges throughout. Earnings were minimal because key operating aspects like production, storage, sales and promotion were not stable most of the time, even though the branding was well received by the public. Response from the single mothers themselves was lukewarm, perhaps because it was not what they were looking for. Although we tried to improve across the years, the lack of resources/funding continued to be an issue. Bella also found it hard to work with potential investors due to diverging visions. However, on social media, it was garnering a lot of positive responses because the concept was novel and innovative at the time. We also managed to work with big brands like agnès b., Lane Crawford and The One Mall.

How do you hope this project will influence viewers?

There seems to be no clear boundary between commercial, art, business and social projects. None of these are independent – they are all interrelated and intersect with one another. We always strive to respond to social issues, reexamine ourselves and be responsible to society, both as designers and a commercial entity. And we believe this has to become a trend and direction for all of us.

Hi! Hill

How/why did you decide to work on the brief?

The project was set in the old Chuen Lung Village, including its abandoned school, and spoke to our love for similar art events/exhibitions in Japan.

What were your key considerations overall when it came to working on this project?

On top of the event identity and promotional materials, we also needed to design a signage system that could guide visitors through the various artworks scattered in different locations across the village. We were also asked to curate an engagement activity for the event. In doing so, our key question was: "How can our designs interact properly with the environment and people of the village, as well as visitors from outside?"

What was your creative starting point for this project? Where did you find your inspiration from?

We actually started with the signage system design. To harmonise the signage with the environment, we began by referencing the habits and objects typically found in the villagers' homes like water pipes, bird cages, and the way they hung their clothes outdoors. However, our first attempt didn't work out because what we did blended in too well with the environment and became 'invisible'. Later on, we developed the identity design based on the characters of the Chinese event name — 山 (hill), 川 (river), and 人 (people), turning the vertical and horizontal strokes of 山 and 川 into destination and directional signs. We also played with a bright yellow colour, so that the minimally designed signs could be seen easily within the relatively chaotic environment of the village. Our engagement programme was inspired by the Chuen Lung river in the village. Although there were health and safety issues stopping us from playing with the river water, we came up with the idea of exchanging water bottles as a means to share experiences with others.

What were the challenges you had to overcome in the course of completing this project?

When it came to the installations, the super-minimal design became one of the challenges. The simple figures/combination of lines were difficult to install at the relatively rough/raw and varied backdrop. Also, because this was not something permanent, we could only make use of existing materials that would not harm the current landscape.

How do you hope this project will influence viewers?

We hope that the unique and inspiring experience offered by this event would increase people's enthusiasm in arts and heritage sites (particularly the less-popular ones), thus help in advancing the development of both.

GREENLITTLE

I SECOND.

#LEILA KONG 唐寧
Artiste 藝人

GREENLADIES

I SECOND.

#JANET LAU 劉汝君
Yoga Teacher 瑜珈導師

GREEN LADIES & GREEN LITTLE

Green Ladies is a social eco enterprise that sets out to achieve environmental and social change through fashion reuse as well as promote employment for middle-aged ladies. Its sub-brand, Green Little, expands this philosophy further into the kidswear market. In conjunction with the launch of its new shop in 2016, CoDesign revamped its visual identity and retail experience, on top of planning and executing an advocacy campaign for the two brands.

SPECIAL FEATURE – CODESIGN

PRICE
時尚价签

8000
TYPES 種

Over 8,000 different synthetic chemicals
are used to make textiles. Many of them
are discharged in freshwater which
significantly lead to water pollution.

全球就纺织品的生産就要採用
8,000 種合成化學物，其中大部分
排放到污水系統造成環境污染。

(非·邑) S2GREENLADIES

Rope Picnic grey
w/bead
HK$ 86.00

PRICE
時尚价签

50
PIECES 件

Toys are at children's fingertips, 65.8% of parents
point out that their children own more than 50 pieces
of toys. Giving your kids too many toys will make
them not learning how to cherish.

玩具對於孩子小來說是唾手是唾手
可得，65.8%家長父母指子女擁有
超過50件或以上玩具，小朋友擁有
過多玩具，令他們不懂得珍惜。

(非·邑) S2GREENLITTLE

S Uniqlo BE floral
shoulder strap
HK$ 38.00

Green Ladies & Green Little

How/why did you decide to work on the brief?

As there were already four Green Ladies stores, we wanted to see what we could do with the Green Little brand. Fundamentally, their proposal matched our own values — it wasn't just about discouraging unnecessary consumption, but also supporting middle-aged women working in fashion, a field that is typically ageist.

What were your key considerations overall when it came to working on this project?

At the beginning, Green Ladies wanted to rid themselves of the poor image second-hand fashion/stores typically have, and hoped to look smarter/trendier. But after several years, people began to forget about the social cause they originally stood for.

Due to their cause, they gained a lot of support from local celebrities, well-known artists and singers, who indirectly promoted their brand/stores by donating a lot of good quality products. However, the low pricing of their products also led to a problem they could not have predicted — because the products were affordable, people ended up 'fighting' for them, which went against Green Ladies' original cause. Therefore, they needed a turning point in their communication to reiterate their original concept and mission.

Our solution was to create a better yet meaningful shopping experience by adding environmental protection info onto their products and shop interiors in a playful tone. For example, the highlighted numbers on the price tags did not refer to the price of the products, but the amount of chemicals that harmed the environment during the production process. We also placed a slogan inside the shop that served to remind customers to think twice about their purchases, telling them instead about the stories behind the clothes. We took advantage of the 'gap' between buying and not buying to tell them that there are more important things to think about.

Besides engaging influencers, commercial models, and celebrities, we also featured ordinary yet socially conscientious people as models to give the brand a more down-to-earth and friendly image. This also allowed the brand messaging to be more palatable. We then took videos of them sharing their personal views on buying second-hand clothes.

Besides engaging influencers, commercial models, and celebrities, we also featured ordinary people as models to give the brand a more down-to-earth and friendly image. This also allowed the brand messaging to be more palatable. We then took videos of them sharing their personal views on buying second-hand clothes.

What was your creative starting point for this project? Where did you find your inspiration from?

In addition to research, we also went around observing how women generally shop. We wanted to find something small/intimate to make use of about the shopping process to promote green messages by integrating them into the shopping experience, rather than just putting slogans in the shop.

What were the challenges you had to overcome in the course of completing this project?

We had to understand our client's limitations well and how limited their resources were, then explore smarter ways to achieve effective results.

How do you hope this project will influence viewers?

We hope that they will have a second thought before purchasing and think of the impact of their actions.

I'MPERFECT

I'MPERFECT is an ongoing movement that hopes to encourage the appreciation of imperfections in the things we use, the people around us, as well as ourselves. Through global partnerships, CoDesign works to consciously improve the use of our limited resources and relationships to create a greener and more harmonious society.

I'MPERFECT MUG

I'MPERFECT PENCIL

I'MPERFECT NOTEBOOK

I'MPERFECT BOOK

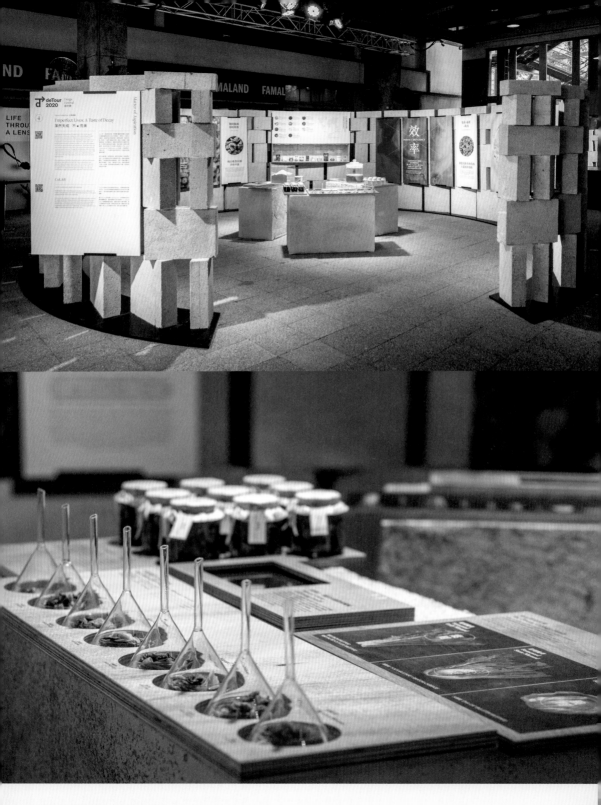

I'MPERFECT

How/why did you decide to work on the brief?

It started off as a commercial project for Loveramics, a ceramics brand in Hong Kong (China) in 2010. We were invited to join their artist series and design surface graphics for their ceramic products. Although we weren't very interested initially, as we began to understand their production process, the high defective rates resulting from it, as well as the ways with which they managed their defective products (if they were not good for recycling or sold at a cheap price, they simply ended up in landfills), we decided to rethink what we could do for these detective products and discussed this with Loveramics instead.

What were your key considerations overall when it came to working on this project?

After visiting their factory in China to have a look at these defective products, we realised that although they did not pass quality checks, the defects were usually not very serious, like an inconsistent paint job or tiny coal marks made by the burning process. We also noticed a signboard in the factory about 'pursuing zero flaws', which led us to think further about why flaws would be such a bad thing.

What was your creative starting point for this project? Where did you find your inspiration from?

Hung: I started to think about the word 'perfect' and suddenly came up with the idea of its opposite, 'imperfect'. I then added an apostrophe in between the letters 'i' and 'm' which gave it another meaning: 'I'm perfect'. I think perfection is very subjective and conditional — everyone has different perspectives and standards, and everything can be interpreted in different ways. Imperfection is original and unique. It's why we look for improvements; a good motivation to get better.

What were the challenges you had to overcome in the course of completing this project?

The key to this project/process was the fact that the original brief was a commercial one, but we turned it into something beyond that with meaning/added value. We have to find where the potential lies and define ourselves and what we should be doing, rather than simply follow the given brief. We can always propose a 'profitable' idea with added value.

How do you hope this project will influence viewers?

Our celebration of imperfection has already gone beyond this project. Our latest project, the I'MPERFECT LIVES Exhibition which was held at PMQ (Hong Kong, China) in November 2020, was about probiotics. People are typically very sensitive to the word 'bacteria', but little do they know that there are lots of good bacteria too. Today, we've just lost our balance between both sides. For example, most of the elderly people in Japan are healthy because their diet contains a lot of good bacteria like 'natto' and fermented yeast. Unfortunately, our modern diets include food with high oil and fat content — which is the bad bacteria.

That's why we set out to 'repackage' the image of bacteria by collaborating with different parties and hosting workshops with them. For example, our I'mperfect Lives Fermentation Workshop Series featured a local farmer making his favourite pickled vegetables, while VEGGIE LABO, a Japanese plant-based grocery store and cooking lab, taught us how to make 'koji' rice. Although bacteria usually looks like something that creates imperfect conditions for humans, it doesn't. Bacteria (the good ones at least) can actually be helpful and assist us in living a better life. We hope people understand that 'our perfection lies in our imperfections'.

SOWGOOD!

SOWGOOD! Positive Education Centre is the first centre in Hong Kong (China) to promote positive mind-sets through experiential learning activities. As part of its philosophy, the centre believes that the strength of an individual child lays the foundation for a life full of flourish. Similar to the cultivation of a plant, a good future is the result of healthy seeding. CoDesign introduced the vision of the project not only through its brand name, but also its logo design, which houses the Chinese word "品" referring to 'character'. Ten 'fruit-tos' were created to illustrate the ten core positive values to children in an interesting and engaging way.

For The People

Dialogue with Founder & Creative Director
Jason Little

Whether it is crippling self-doubt or the 'impostor syndrome' that is finally being recognised as a real thing, building a career in the creative field can often be a journey of constant questioning at any level. Working on briefs that one does not particularly believe in can often chip away at one's reality, resulting in the need for a wake-up call of sorts — whether it comes from the outside or within. The team at For The People know all too well what this feels like, with many of them having run major, international branding studios in their past lives. Today, they are multi-format storytellers that wear their hearts on their sleeves to 'care about each other' and work on things worth doing for others. The following Q&A with the studio's founder Jason Little captures snippets of their design process and studio philosophies.

MIMI LEUNG

THE BATTLE 13/02/2020

THE BATTLE 13/02/2020

MULGA

KRIS ANDREW SMALL

THE BATTLE 13/02/2020

THE BATTLE 13/02/2020

CRAIG & KARL

THE BATTLE 13/02/2020

ILANA BODENSTEIN

THE BATTLE 13/02/2020

JEREMY LORD

MULGA 13

JEREMY

SPECIAL FEATURE — FOR THE PEOPLE

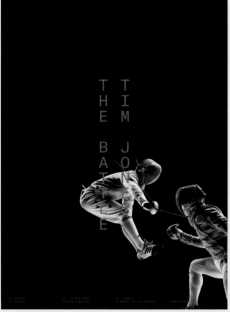

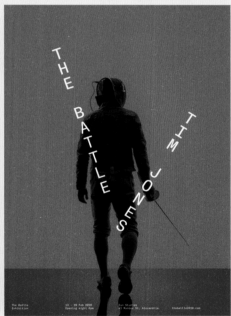

THE BATTLE

The Battle is an annual exhibition that channels Australia's love of sport to financially support important, meaningful work done by select charities and not-for-profits. The inaugural Battle exhibition consisted of two parts — a photographic exploration of the enigmatic sport of fencing by Tim Jones, alongside an artistic collaboration exploring the art of the fencing mask. All profits raised from sales went towards the Chris O'Brien Lifehouse cancer hospital. For The People designed an identity that leaned into the photography, balancing it with a subtle typographic nod to the foil/sabre weapon.

How did your design career begin?

Starting For The People was an ambition I'd had for years. A studio that would carry forward the best aspects of the various studios I'd worked at whilst also attempting to improve on some of the things that didn't necessarily work well. At the heart of the studio, is the desire to enable people to work on the type of work they aspire to work on, with clients who have the ambition to push boundaries and challenge the status quo of their categories.

For our team, it's a place that doesn't compartmentalise people into a strict title or role, enabling individuals to shape their own roles and lean in to their strengths and areas of focus. Over the years, the studio has become a collective of smart and engaged people, with a continuous exchange of ideas between strategists, storytellers and designers. Essentially, every person within the studio can author the work and play a critical role in the outcome.

What is your definition of 'design for good'?

At For The People, it's about creating and balancing both social and economic value for our clients. It's work that's worth doing, and is work that's joyful. Doing great work takes a lot of motivation and passion — to maintain it, we work with companies and organisations that wish to be a force for good (either by making genuinely meaningful improvements to the lives of others, or simply brightening somebody's day).

I believe brands are driven by relationships first, economics second — because brands are for, about, and powered by people. Because of this, we can only build trust if we understand that social value is of greater importance than financial value — and not the other way around.

What inspired you to focus your design skills for good?

When you have the skills and means to make a difference, then it becomes an obligation to use these to drive positive change. The opportunity comes from being an independent studio. We have the power to choose who we work for and how we utilise our time.

For The People is a collection of highly engaged individuals, and each one of those people has a say about the work they do and for whom — and so the decision is a simple one. Society faces many challenges, such as climate change, marriage equality, domestic violence, animal abuse, racial equality, homelessness, indigenous reconciliation and so on. We're able to use our collective skills and resources to work on many of these areas.

What do you hope to achieve through your projects?

Our work is intended to make life better. We want to make sure what our people do within our walls broadens and improves their own life experience and that of our clients. We want to enable organisations to be the best they can be, and equip them with the tools and know-how to take them forward successfully.

How has designing for good improved your skills as a designer, and changed you as a human being?

No matter how long I've been designing, I've never managed to shake the insecurities and the imposter syndrome that is common within our field of work. But, working with clients that make a difference in this world has provided a counter point to this question of self-worth. I've seen huge changes take place with organisations I've worked with, where they've evolved and grown to achieve success beyond their original ambitions. The working relationships we've developed during and after the process have brought a huge amount of joy to my life, and many of my clients have become lifelong friends. I have a far greater level of empathy and understanding thanks to these kinds of projects, along with a very different outlook on life.

How do you think designers can change the world through their work? What values, skills, or experiences would they need to have?

Some designers can change the world — that's very true. For others, that change comes through working with clients who are actively focused on changing the world. The ability to do this kind of work starts with empathy. Experience allows you to understand the business and organisational challenges that design can solve. But anyone can make a difference by having a positive mindset and the desire to do something about it. We all share a responsibility to make this world a better place.

What's a day in your studio like?

The day begins with a team catchup, usually virtual, due to the global pandemic and the location of some of our team members across different cities in Australia. This meeting sets up the the workload for everyone. We run through a list of jobs, and update the rest of the studio on the current state of projects — what's happening specifically on that day, the critical deadlines, meetings or issues to solve and so forth. From there, each project team usually assembles soon after for a quick huddle to review work, ensure everyone is clear on what they're doing, and get cracking.

As a highly-functioning collaborative team, each person in the studio will wear multiple hats on any given day. This means there is involvement at every stage of a project, from the research and strategic phases, through to the delivery of the work, with obvious specialisms coming into play, i.e. storytellers focusing more on writing, designers taking a lot of the responsibility around visual expression. Everyone has client interactions and a responsibility to the rest of the team to push the work as far as we can; and keep each project moving. Each of us will have at least two or three projects running at any one time.

"...anyone can make a difference by having a positive mindset and the desire to do something about it."

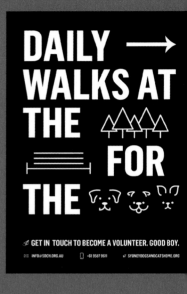

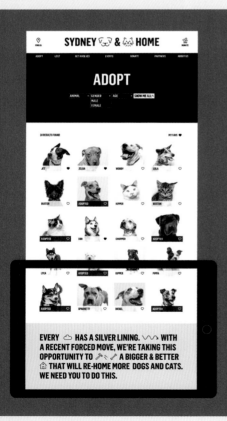

SYDNEY DOGS & CATS HOME

As a not-for-profit animal shelter, Sydney Dogs & Cats Home rehomes over 3,000 animals each year. To give the animals the best possible chance of finding a new home, For The People studio elevated each animal to celebrity status — complete with glamorous photos that captured their true quirks. The logo itself is made up of interchangeable dog and cat icons, with one generated for every animal that arrives at the shelter. With each potential pet having its 15 minutes of fame, the shelter has a brand that centres around the positivity of adoption.

WOMEN'S AND GIRLS' EMERGENCY CENTRE (WAGEC)

WAGEC offers shelter and support to women and children who are at-risk, as well as victims of domestic violence and homelessness. In recent years, they had been struggling to clearly express who they are, leading to a lack of awareness and the credibility necessary to encourage much-needed funding when in fact, they empower survivors. For The People helped them to define a visual language that strikes a clear stance, harking back to its grassroots beginnings and its philosophy about women supporting women.

Women's and Girls' Emergency Centre

How/why did you decide to work on the brief?

It had been 40 years since the not-for-profit, Women's and Girls' Emergency Centre (WAGEC) was founded in the Sydney suburb of Redfern. Growing out of a broken system, the shelter was built off grassroots activism, bringing women together to help those in need.

Fast forward to now, and WAGEC are still fighting for women's access to safety, housing, and other basic needs. When they approached us in 2019, they explained how their identity struggled to capture the extent of who they were, as well as what they did. With little visibility, they were unable to create the awareness necessary to encourage much needed funding.

After the initial meeting, it was impossible to say no to an organisation with an incredible purpose, but a lack of means to deliver on it as effectively as they needed. Once we understood the following statistics, it only strengthened our resolve.

· Domestic violence is the biggest cause of homelessness for women.
· On average per week, one woman is murdered in Australia by a current or former partner.
· In 2015, 279,000 Australians sought help from homelessness services, out of which 60% were women.
· Australian police deal with domestic violence every two minutes.

What were your key considerations overall when it came to working on this project?

When we do work for organisations like this, we don't take the task lightly. WAGEC is doing challenging work to help victims of domestic violence and homelessness. That means we have to understand the sensitivities about the subject matter and the real challenges the organisation faces around awareness and revenue generation. Our team invested large amounts of time and energy into thoroughly understanding the origins and current situation of the shelter, and how to best help them.

The relationship we would have to have with this client was critical. It needed to be completely open and trustworthy, so that everything we developed would be of true value to them and solve real needs. The project needed to give them a clear path forward as an organisation, with the tools and assets provided to enable them to deliver on their needs on an ongoing basis.

What was your creative starting point for this project? Where did you find your inspiration from?

WAGEC aims to raise awareness around domestic violence leading to homelessness, and provide hope and shelter for those in need. They go against the prevailing view that women in need are powerless victims, when in fact they are empowered survivors. The organisation is striking a clear stance around this misunderstood area, harking back to its grassroots beginnings. Our starting point was when we gained clarity about the organisa-tion: WAGEC is about women supporting women.

The identity responds to the greater community of women and drives a conversation and understanding about supporting each other and building a community of assistance. The new logo responds to the urgency of their work, a shelter that points women to that critical piece of information in times of need.

What were the challenges you had to overcome in the course of completing this project?

Like any not-for-profit, the ability to communicate visually is key to building awareness and understanding of their services. We encouraged WAGEC to avoid the usual tropes of charity photography and the often generic stock imagery of shelters — used in order to protect and respect the anonymity of the people who have relied on the services.

Instead, the organisation is now using contemporary illustration as a key aspect of the brand. To kick things off, we created 'We're the Women', an art exhibition that captured the heart of the organisation — women supporting women. 16 leading female illustrators from around Australia each donated a bespoke artwork that celebrated WAGEC's approach to working with women and families in crisis. Signed and numbered art prints were sold at the exhibition to raise funds, whilst also providing an imagery library for the brand across applications.

How do you hope this project will influence viewers?

To summarise the intent of this project and what it hoped to achieve, Helen Silvia, Chief Executive Officer of WAGEC wrote this —

"We stand for gender equity, social justice, the elimination of gendered-based violence in our community, and the safety and security for all women and children. Our new brand direction has been created with respect and collaboration, and will most importantly allow Women's and Girls' Emergency Centre to amplify our voice in the community to raise awareness for things that matter to us — to all of us."

We're picking up what you're putting down

Moving out or cleaning up? Each household is entitled to 4 free booked clean ups.

Council Clean-Up

Inner West Council offers free collection for damaged household items. Your area has 2 scheduled Clean Ups per year.

Find the dates for your street via
— Online waste calendar
— Download our Inner West Waste App

INNER WEST
02 9392 5863
innerwest.nsw.gov.au

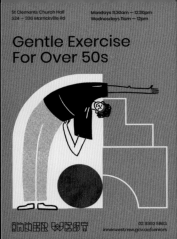

St Clements Church Hall
S34 — 336 Marrickville Rd

Mondays 11:30am — 12:30pm
Wednesdays 11am — 12pm

Gentle Exercise For Over 50s

INNER WEST
02 9392 5863
innerwest.nsw.gov.au/seniors

Limited Spots
Leichhardt Park Aquatic Centre

Every Saturday
9am — 10pm

Prenatal Yoga Courses

INNER WEST
02 9392 5863
innerwest.nsw.gov.au

INNER WEST

The visual identity for Sydney's Inner West region was designed to capture the spirit of its creative community, while representing the vibrant and diverse neighbourhoods living side-by-side in harmony. For The People created a system around the iconic places, spaces and historic architecture in the area, with intentional flexibility injected to allow for multiple configurations to be generated from the graphic shapes. The outcome provides a framework for all communications, events and community.

SPECIAL FEATURE — FOR THE PEOPLE

Inner West

How/why did you decide to work on the brief?

Following a merger of three councils in Sydney's Inner West, a new identity was required to unify the region. With many of the team members living and working in the region, and having worked on similar projects for city councils across Australia, we were engaged by the newly formed council to develop the work.

What were your key considerations overall when it came to working on this project?

The identity needed to capture the Inner West's uniquely creative community and represent the vibrant and diverse neighbourhoods living side-by-side in harmony. It would provide a framework for all communications, local events and community programmes, whilst instilling pride in the local communities. Therefore, the identity had to have built-in flexibility within the system to communicate a whole range of needs for different audiences, whilst also capturing the creative and cultural mashups that characterise the region.

What was your creative starting point for this project? Where did you find your inspiration from?

As one of the older areas in Sydney, the Inner West has a long and varied history, having been constantly reshaped and repurposed by a range of people across classes and industry divides. Because of this, many places in the Inner West have, by necessity, been creatively reimagined many times, using existing structures in new and inventive ways. This formed the start of the identity, which leaned heavily into characteristics embedded in spaces and buildings that capture the personality and history of the Inner West.

What were the challenges you had to overcome in the course of completing this project?

With projects designed to be used by the community, there are numerous challenges around the intuitive nature of the design system. To this end, we had to ensure there was enough structure to keep things simple, but with enough flex for ongoing usage over time.

One of the key challenges was the process around the word mark, which changed on several occasions after community consultation sessions and feedback. The final outcome is a word mark that has multiple configurations based on the different physical spaces of the Inner West. These individual elements are used across communications to house content, and create a clear and coherent brand whilst ensuring there is ample space for creative interpretation by the in-house team and the many creative collaborators with the city.

How do you hope this project will influence viewers?

This is an identity borne of place. With community consultation playing a big role in the development of the work, the end result needed to match people's expectations, have the ability to evolve over time alongside ever-evolving neighbourhoods, and create opportunities for greater engagement between them and the council. A key ambition was to resonate with the community and build a sense of local pride.

ADOBE PAWTRAITS

Adobe Pawtraits was a seasonal campaign to engage students and educate them on the benefits of Adobe's Creative Cloud tools and subscriptions by showing them how applications like Lightroom and Photoshop can help them create the perfect pet portraits. A collaboration with the Sydney Dogs and Cats Home, the team at For The People set out to raise awareness of animals needing adoption, focusing on exposing the inner beauty of shelter animals by encouraging people to see these animals as the perfect complement to their lives.

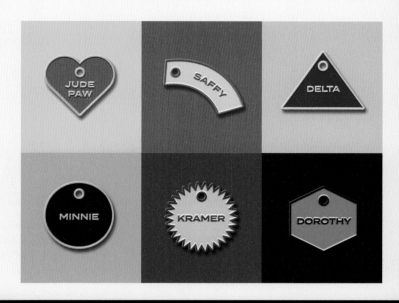

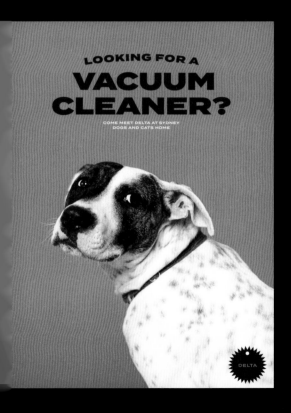

LOOKING FOR A VACUUM CLEANER?

COME MEET DELTA AT SYDNEY DOGS AND CATS HOME

DELTA

① **AUTOMATICALLY PICKS UP ALL FOOD SCRAPS**

② **QUIET ENOUGH TO OPERATE LATE INTO THE NIGHT WITHOUT DISTURBING NEIGHBOURS**

③ **REVOLUTIONARY BAGLESS SYSTEM**

④ **AUTO-SLEEP FUNCTION**

Adobe × SYDNEY 🐾&🐾 HOME

LOOKING FOR A
NEW THERAPIST?
COME MEET JUDE PAW AT SYDNEY DOGS AND CATS HOME

JUDE PAW

UNWAVERINGLY-ATTENTIVE LISTENER

LITERALLY CAN'T BREAK CLIENT-THERAPIST CONFIDENTIALITY

NEVER TAKES ANYONE ELSE'S SIDE

DOESN'T REALLY MIND IF YOUR COMPLAINING BECOMES REPETITIVE

LOOKING FOR A
BINGE-WATCH BUDDY?
COME MEET CASEY AT SYDNEY DOGS AND CATS HOME

YOUR FAVOURITE SHOW IS ALWAYS HER FAVOURITE SHOW

ALWAYS HAPPY TO CANCEL PLANS IN FAVOUR OF A NIGHT ON THE COUCH

WON'T JUDGE YOU SNACKING

DOESN'T HAVE ANYWHERE TO BE TOMORROW

LOOKING FOR A
PERSONAL TRAINER?
COME MEET KRAMER AT SYDNEY DOGS AND CATS HOME

KRAMER

ALWAYS IN THE MOOD FOR A RUN

WON'T BODY-SHAME YOU

CAN LURE YOU OUT THE DOOR WITH LITERAL PUPPY DOG EYES

HEARTILY ENCOURAGES POST-WORKOUT FISH AND CHIPS

LOOKING FOR AN
ALARM CLOCK?
COME MEET DOROTHY AT SYDNEY DOGS AND CATS HOME

DOROTHY

DOESN'T HAVE A SNOOZE BUTTON

AUTOMATICALLY ADJUSTS TO DAYLIGHT SAVING

DOESN'T NEED TO BE PLUGGED IN

LESS NOISY (BUT MORE FUN) THAN TYPICAL ALARM TONES

ADOBE PAWTRAITS

MINNIE

#AdobePawtrai

SPECIAL FEATURE – FOR THE PEOPLE

Adobe Pawtraits

How/why did you decide to work on the brief?

We've worked with Adobe on several projects over the years. When they came to us with this project, they were looking to engage with student audiences in Australia and APAC around their reduced price Creative Cloud product subscription. A key challenge was to create a compelling reason to trial the applications and build greater engagement with the brand. With quite an open brief, we were confident we could do something a little unexpected and worthwhile.

What were your key considerations overall when it came to working on this project?

How could we build social value in the work? What would motivate audiences to get involved and build greater engagement around the offering? We wanted to push beyond simply selling the product, and so we suggested partnering with a previous not-for-profit client of ours, Sydney Dogs and Cats Home. Working with this animal shelter allowed us to not only promote the Adobe Suite, but actually put the Adobe tools to good use — to help animals get adopted.

What was your creative starting point for this project? Where did you find your inspiration from?

When we designed the visual identity for Sydney Dogs and Cats Home several years ago, we recognised that showing the shelter animals in their best light was the key to adoption, instead of imagery that used pity as the mechanism. A good photo can go a long way in helping a pet find a home by capturing their true personality and showing how they could easily fit into your life.

We worked with amateur animal photographer James Dore to show how Adobe tools like Lightroom and Photoshop could turn a good image into the perfect portrait. The brand campaign raised awareness of the animals needing adoption whilst helping students create a 'perfect pawtrait' of an animal in their life. Communications focused on exposing the inner beauty of some of their most overlooked lodgers, encouraging people to see these animals as the perfect complement to their lives.

What were the challenges you had to overcome in the course of completing this project?

The target market comprised students across APAC. This was one key challenge, in that we had to create work that could resonate with different audiences from different cultures. An obvious challenge was meeting the actual target numbers to make the campaign a success. In a way, we were using the marketing campaign as a vehicle for doing good.

The most difficult challenge, though, was the production requirements around photographing animals — specifically ones that had come from difficult or abusive backgrounds. This was something that had to be managed carefully, which is why we gave the handlers from the shelter the capacity to ensure the environment and process was the best it could be for the animals.

How do you hope this project will influence viewers?

Every animal has its own unique personality, and deserves a life of love and respect. If this project helped to reinforce this idea and give people a better understanding of both shelter animals and their own pets, then the project was a success.

DERWENT VALLEY

Regarded as one of Tasmania's last great secrets, the Derwent Valley brims with the 'biggests', 'deepests', 'wildests', and 'weirdests'. Inspired by the fable-like qualities of the region, For The People designed a new identity by collating and sharing its unbelievable yet true(-ish) tales with the world. Using classic literary aesthetics, from illustrations to storytelling, and basing the core brand around 9 key icons, the team designed a brand that engaged and amplified the thousands of voices that call 'The Valley' home.

CASE STUDIES

Ⓔ Environment

As the implications from climate change slowly begin to impact our world, good by design is about going greener to protect the planet.

Ⓗ Health & Well-being

From advocating for better mental health to raising awareness on diseases unseen, good by design is about promoting more empathy.

Ⓢ Social Activism

Good by design is about being bold and making a stand on the right side of history so we can each rise up and make collective change happen.

Ⓒ Community-building

Whether it is improving social architecture or getting to know our neighbours better, good by design is about bringing people together.

Ⓓ Education

Knowledge is the key to progress, which is why good by design is about equipping and empowering us to shape a brighter future.

Cori Corinne

Dress.Code.

Dress.Code. is a series of 112 portraits reflecting on the societal scrutiny of women, as well as the non-binary individual's self-expression and physical form. Designer Cori Corinne embarked on the project to help us visualise our fragmented and compartmentalised identities in the process of adapting to those who seek to define us in our everyday lives. Accompanied by their written personal reflections, each participant was captured head-on in powerful images that were showcased in an online gallery set up to celebrate our individualism and shared experiences. Through the project, Cori hopes to help us recognise ourselves in a diverse community declaring space as our own — defining our identities and deciding on our own dress code.

TRASH ARTIFACTS. RAZORS. BRAS. JEANS WE'VE KEPT FOR YEARS DREAMING OF OUR PAST SIZE. SUNSCREEI SHAPEWEAR. TORN OUT IMAGERY HE IDEAL WOMAN. S. PINK BEJEWELED MIRRORS. CONTRAPTIONS FOR THOSE OF US WITH BREASTS TOO BIG FOR THE STANDARD STRAPLESS.

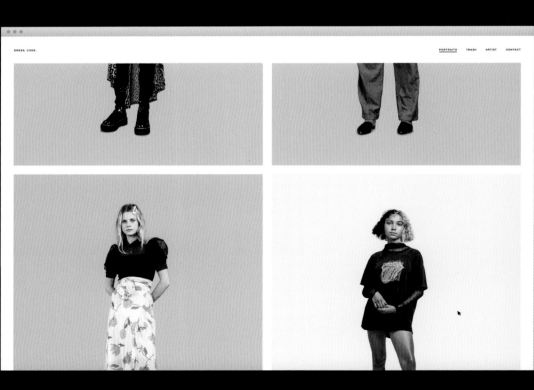

Could you please elaborate on your research/development process? How important is it in the overall scheme of things and how do your findings influence the final design work?

No matter the project, the process is the foundation of everything that I do. The process behind Dress.Code. was unique to the project, as it revolved around the personal experiences and identities of each individual. The research phase spanned a little over 2 months, where I reached out to people in the community and met with each person individually. I wanted to get to know them intimately and for them to see that speaking with me was a safe space. The only way to do that was for me to be just as vulnerable, sharing my personal experiences as a woman and the reasons I pursued this series. Some meetings lasted an hour while others lasted 3 to 4 hours. Not everyone decided to be part of the series, but each person influenced my journey and need to continue. No matter the outcome, the development process was the core of the series.

How do you typically work and communicate with your client or overcome differences in opinion to achieve the best results? Following which, what do you hope to inspire/change in audiences from this project?

Most people are visual learners, especially when it comes to explaining a creative experience. That means that verbal debates or explanations are irrelevant. Instead, I take the time to visualise what a client is expressing, alongside a visual of what I believe to be the most effective way to visualise the idea. Once you have both visuals, you are able to efficiently and effectively discuss about the differences while talking through the pros and cons of both expressions. The client learns from you and you learn from the client. In the same way I work with typical design clients, I brought that process of visualisation to Dress.Code. in bringing the series to life.

How do the skills/abilities of a designer come into play, particularly in projects for the greater good? What have you personally learned/taken away from this project?

The Dress.Code project helped to define me not only as a designer, but an artist with social intent. I have been on a journey trying to understand who I am as a creative, reflecting on the differences of my process as an artist versus a designer. During Dress.Code., the intent and conceptual aspect of the process felt like I was pulling from my roots as an artist, but the way I framed, visualised and shared the work was through my lens as a designer. A designer has the ability to communicate abstract, and at times, sensitive subjects we recognise either consciously or subconsciously as a society. Designers communicate these ideas in a way that anyone can retain and reflect on.

There have been rising discussions on designers' roles and responsibilities over the years. What do you think is/are the core values/mentality designers today need to be equipped with in order to foster a better world?

Identifying as a designer is not just an industry label to reflect my career. My work, no matter how I label it, is woven into my life. It's hard for me create anything without core values that relate to who I am as a human being and what's important to me. Inclusivity. Sustainability. Community. I believe it's important no matter what type of creative you are, to have an awareness of what is happening in the world around you and what type of influence you can have with your work. I find that self-initiated projects are where I have the complete freedom to dive into that influence.

CASE STUDIES

Out of the Box

CLIENT
Samsung

Special Projects were approached in 2009 to look for solutions as to why not enough old people were using smart phones. To discover what the hindrance was, the team undertook an unconventional research journey to draw knowledge from their everyday experiences and pick up contextual cues. Upon discovering that phone manuals were the main issue, they designed a beautifully crafted, easy-to-understand guide that served as an analogue bridge between the elderly and what they deemed an 'unfriendly' topic, technology, to empower them to pick up their phones more often. 'Out of the Box' has since been exhibited at MoMa in New York and in Vienna as part of the Design Diversity exhibition.

Place
your
phone
here

n your phonebook
our phonebook
nebook

You're all set!
For instructions on
using the phone have
a look at the Using
your Samsung Tocco
Lite book.

"Design evolves as the rest of the world constantly changes, and it is clear that our role as designers now is shifting from people-centered design to planet-centered design."

Could you please elaborate on your research/development process? How important is it in the overall scheme of things and how do your findings influence the final design work?

For 'Out of the Box', we spent a lot of time designing a research methodology to engage older adults and help us understand their needs and aspirations. One-on-one home visits and group workshops were carried out in the UK, Norway and Italy to help the design team get a first-hand perspective on the problems experienced by older users. These insights showed us that older adults wanted to use all the technology available to them — and they were keen to learn from the right prompts.

Put the SIM card here.

Contents

How do you typically work and communicate with your clients or overcome differences in opinion to achieve the best results? Following which, what do you hope to inspire/change in audiences from this project?

We aim to take our clients on a journey with us throughout the research and ideation process. We use rich imagery and document every step of the process and try to help the client clearly see the decision process we have gone through, so by the time the concept is revealed, they are usually completely onside. In this particular project the main thing we hoped to communicate was the discovery that the majority of older adults do not need or want a 'special phone' — they want the same

phone as everyone else. The challenge therefore transformed from designing a special phone to helping people understand how to use their new phone.

How do the skills/abilities of a designer come into play, particularly in projects for the greater good? What have you personally learned/taken away from this project?

There are so many problems in the world which deserve to be understood thoughtfully and respectfully. The role of the designer is to find out what those problems truly are, and propose solutions which genuinely solve that problem for the audience experiencing it.

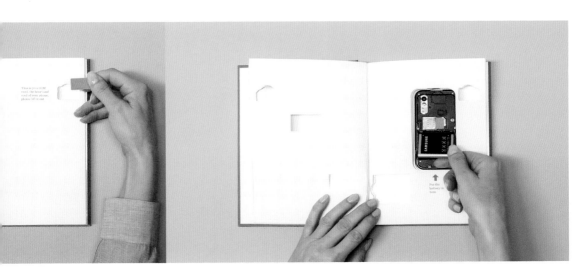

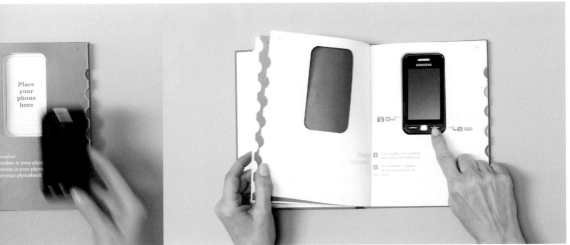

Balisa

Balisa is a therapeutic tool that accompanies and supports the healing process of adult survivors of child sexual abuse, where a series of pieces are provided to facilitate communication between psychologist and survivor by representing the emotions experienced during the healing process. Each emotion is linked to a piece and stacked together to form a totem that the person takes home, so they can follow their emotional management and define their own safety zone. In creating the tool, designer Ariadna collaborated with survivors and psychologists specialising in the subject to play a part in genuinely contributing to the visibility and communication of this problem in society.

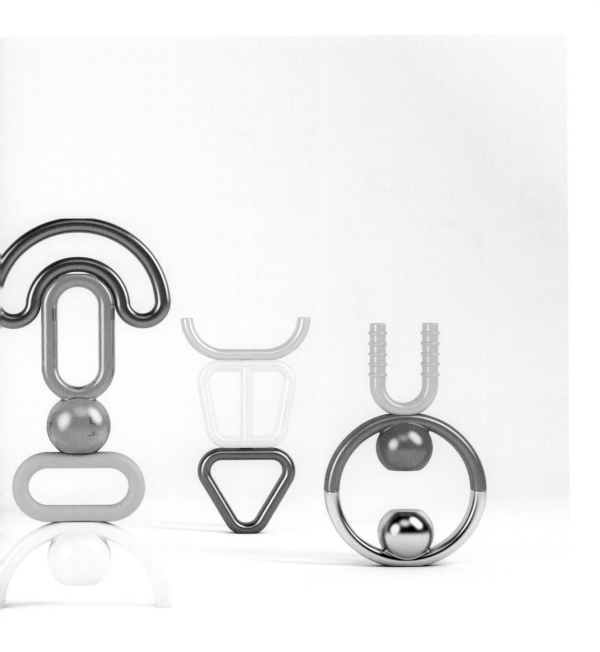

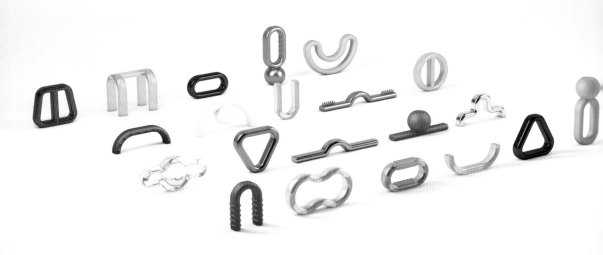

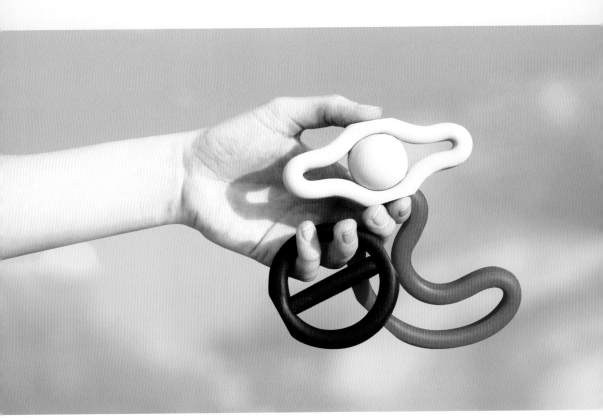

Could you please elaborate on your research/development process? How important is it in the overall scheme of things and how do your findings influence the final design work?

Child sexual abuse is a social problem that affects a large percentage of the population, but instead, they are treated with taboo and secrecy. Personally, design is a very powerful communication tool that allows us to improve problems that affect our society, and it is for this reason that I chose the subject of child sexual abuse, because it needs attention and visibility. Through this project, I learned that the healing process experienced by survivors of the trauma of child sexual abuse is a very hard and long process. It is for this reason that it is highly recommended that they attend psychological therapy, so that the survivor does not have to face this process alone and can follow a path guided by a professional.

How do you typically work and communicate with your client or overcome differences in opinion to achieve the best results? Following which, what do you hope to inspire/change in audiences from this project?

In my opinion, the best way to work or collaborate with a person is through communication. Talk from the beginning about the problem or needs to be solved. During the design process, sharing the process is key in order to design a product that provides real improvement. The main goal of Balisa is to contribute to the visibility and communication of child sexual abuse, so that it is no longer treated with secrecy and taboo. In addition, it aims to facilitate communication between child sexual abuse survivors and psychologists during therapy and support the healing process of adult survivors.

How do the skills/abilities of a designer come into play, particularly in projects for the greater good? What have you personally learned/taken away from this project?

I believe that design has the ability to bring improvements to people and our environment, starting from a critical view of what is happening in the world. This is because design allows us to communicate, make visible and evolve our day by day. Balisa starts from the fact that 1 in 5 children receives some type of abuse before reaching the age of 17. Analysing the number of people affected by this problem, I considered that design could contribute some improvement, encouraging and supporting the survivors of child sexual abuse to go to therapy and start the healing process.

There have been rising discussions on designers' roles and responsibilities over the years. What do you think is/are the core values/mentality designers today need to be equipped with in order to foster a better world?

In my opinion, we design for the people. This means that from the values of oneself, the designer must look towards his environment. A designer should be an empathic, critical and respectful with people and the environment. Apart from this, I believe that to achieve good design, it is important that the designer collaborates with other professionals and with the people to whom the product is being designed. This way, a much more practical and effective result can be achieved.

Kosuke Takahashi Ⓒ

LINKAGE

LINKAGE is a haptic communication game that connects fingers with sticks, through which players have to feel and control their movements by using the power of their fingers to balance the sticks so that the sticks do not fall. In creating the game, product designer Kosuke Takahashi was inspired by haptic sign language, a means of communication mainly used by the deaf and visually impaired to recognise signs by their hands and senses not typically used. By making it into something anyone can play by pushing and pulling with their fingers, he created an accessible game open to all people regardless of disability, nationality, age, or gender.

Could you please elaborate on your research/development process? How important is it in the overall scheme of things and how do your findings influence the final design work?

When we first met our deafblind friend, we were fascinated by the way he would communicate using haptics, a new experience that stimulated senses we had never used before. In the course of getting to know him, he told us that there are not many games today with which the deaf and blind, hearing people as well as sighted people can play together – which led me to start a project creating games inspired by the haptic sign language. As an action, play triggers communication, so by thinking about play in an inclusive way, we could create a world where diverse people can naturally connect and mix.

How do you typically work and communicate with your Client or overcome differences in opinion to achieve the best results? Following which, what do you hope to inspire/change in audiences from this project?

We are contradictory beings who want to be different and yet, at the same time, be the

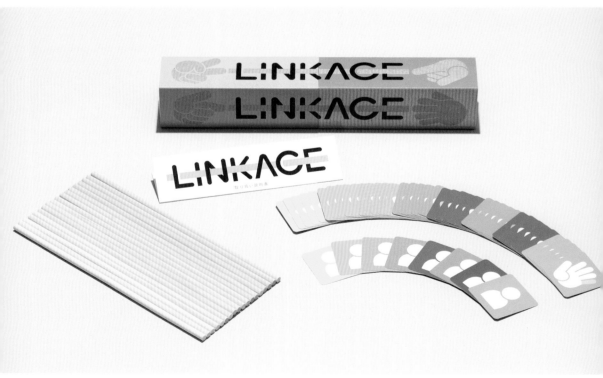

same as others. So, the process of finding common ground while acknowledging our differences was stimulating. In this case, the gist of the project was that my deafblind friend and I could relate to the fun of communicating through haptics. The interesting point of this game is that everyone can get involved in the world of haptic communication and naturally become friends. Through the project, we wanted to increase the number of products out there that allowed for people to mingle naturally, regardless of disability, nationality, age, or gender — and I hope that this idea will spread beyond games.

How do the skills/abilities of a designer come into play, particularly in projects for the greater good? What have you personally learned/taken away from this project?

Collaboration is important and gives us moments to allow an idea to grow outside of the box. For this project, the inspiration came from a friend who told me about the fun of Haptic Sign Language.

Museum of Us

CLIENT
Southwark Council

Fieldwork Facility collaborated
with New London Architecture
to reimagine community consultation through the Museum of
Us, which was piloted in the Old
Kent Road area for Southwark
Council. The Museum of Us was a
campaign, exhibition and project
space, as well as a programme of
events designed to bring together
members of the local community
to tell the stories of its people. To
represent the underrepresented
voices and maximise engagement,
the team commissioned photographer Suki Dhanda to shoot
portraits that the locals could
unequivocally identify with. The
epicentre of the project was a
refurbished shop which was transformed into a positive and democratic space to enable conversations and action on long-term
plans for the area, where people
could share ideas and opinions
about what is truly important in
their community.

231 Old Kent Road
oldkentroad.org.uk/museumof

231 Old Kent Road
oldkentroad.org.uk/museumofus

Could you please elaborate on your research/development process? How important is it in the overall scheme of things and how do your findings influence the final design work?

At Fieldwork Facility we work very hard to deliver the best creative work. We are specialists in not specialising and approach design challenges with open eyes rather than a scripted process, tailoring our process to each challenge. Broadly speaking, each project has four phases.

Phase 1: Discovery. First, we work like detectives, typically spending a lot of time on the ground doing fieldwork, researching, observing, indexing, rummaging through archives, interviewing stakeholders, conducting analogous research experiences etc. to feed the creative engine and ensure we understand the design challenge from all angles. Our research and discovery phase gives us strong foundations to design from and a strategic perspective on the challenge at hand.

Phase 2: Exploration. In our second phase, we synthesise everything from the discovery phase and get started on design concepts. Typically, we create pop-up studios within the community to make sure our work has an affinity with them.

Phase 3: Define. In the latter phases of a project, we craft and develop design — figuring out how turn ideas and sketches into something real and impactful.

Phase 4: Delivery. Finally, all of our design development turns into production plans and specifications, essentially seeing them through to delivery.

How do you typically work and communicate with your Client or overcome differences in opinion to achieve the best results? Following which, what do you hope to inspire/change in audiences from this project?

All of our work is underpinned by rigorous research, conceptual integrity and a crafted execution. It's really rare that we find a big difference in opinion far along into a project. Our process creates really strong groundwork from the outset, underlined by our emphasis on great research and truthful concepts. Also, I think we are very lucky as a studio to have brave clients come to us to do things that haven't been done before.

I like living here because of the

Where should it be easier to get to?

Community Transport

Facilities

history

Pubs

The Old Kent Road area has seen a variety of activity through the years, often featuring around the many public houses that lined the road.

Old Kent Road pubs

FREE EVENT
Historic Pubs Of
The Old Kent Road
Led by Diane Cochrane

What do you
about the ar

Museum of Us

How do the skills/abilities of a designer come into play, particularly in projects for the greater good? What have you personally learned/taken away from this project?

The big idea behind everything we do at Fieldwork Facility is that design is a role of citizenship, meaning before we're designers, we are citizens. Beyond the concept of just living somewhere, citizenship is an interesting idea to me because it implies that you have to be proactive and participate in the communities you live in — and being a part of each of these communities gives me the ability to tackle any design challenge.

There have been rising discussions on designers' roles and responsibilities over the years. What do you think is/are the core values/mentality designers today need to be equipped with in order to foster a better world?

Our 'Museum of Us' project set out to explore how we can create a highly participatory process that reimagines community consultation. Besides creating a campaign. we designed a visual identity that was based around coloured stickers, as they are easy ways to leave your mark on an area or a space. We also commissioned a fantastic photographer named Suki Dhanda to take photos of the people, entering the final portraits into an exhibition. Typically, with these kind of projects there can be a sentiment of 'why are you spending money on that?' — but we kept 67% of the money spent within the area.

Éssers

CLIENT
Ajuntament de València

democràcia estudio developed a campaign to sensitise the population to the importance of the Declaration of Human Rights, while promoting the fact that Valencia, where the studio is based, is an equal and fair city. The team used narrative storytelling to talk about what makes people different from automata, criticising inequalities and their representations via a dichotomy between the analogue and technology. Featuring images from mosaics that, as viewers get closer to the pieces, show blurred human figures and represent colours reminiscent of the pixelation of screens, the colours of the characters eventually make up a range of all the pigments that represent human skin from afar.

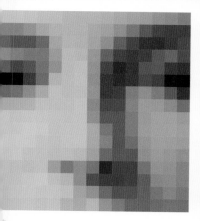

ssers.

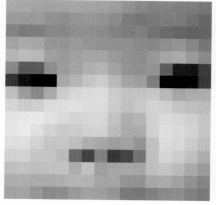

éssers.

10 de desembre
Commemoració de la Declaració
Universal dels Drets Humans

València, ciutat igual, ciutat justa

AJUNTAMENT
DE VALÈNCIA

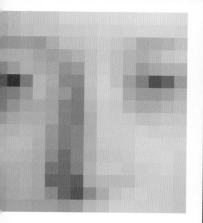

ssers.

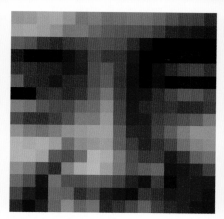

éssers.

10 de desembre
Commemoració de la Declaració
Universal dels Drets Humans

València, ciutat igual, ciutat justa

AJUNTAMENT
DE VALÈNCIA

"As in any profession that has a public projection, any of the work carried out by a designer must have a pedagogical load, which helps to build a better society, in which inequalities are banished."

éssers.
seres.
beings.

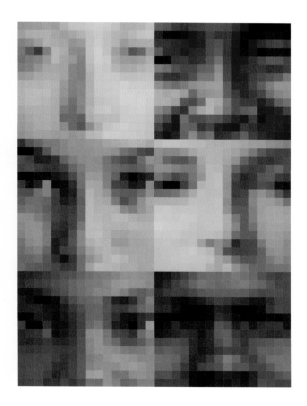

Could you please elaborate on your research/development process? How important is it in the overall scheme of things and how do your findings influence the final design work?

For the Éssers project, our research was based on the contents of the Universal Declaration of Human Rights, from which we learned about what the greatest inequalities in today's society are. As such, we decided to focus on social inequalities, in particular, the inequalities that occur in digital media and social networks.

How do you typically work and communicate with your client or overcome differences in opinion to achieve the best results? Following which, what do you hope to inspire/change in audiences from this project?

When dealing with differences of opinion with clients, what we do is explain the reasons that led us to make our proposal and why we believe it is the best option for them, which usually leads to good results. The Éssers campaign was born to make visible a problem that has haunted us throughout history — one that can unfortunately become greater. Our obligation as citizens is to be aware, raise visibility and denounce any behaviour that may be capable of generating a negative attitude towards inequality.

How do the skills/abilities of a designer come into play, particularly in projects for the greater good? What have you personally learned/taken away from this project?

As in any project, designers must contribute all their skills to achieve the objective(s) desired by the client: in this case, awareness as to the contents of the Universal Declaration of Human Rights. During the creative process, we discovered certain rights that we were unaware of, which will help us take them into account in the future in trying to help eliminate social inequalities.

Pablo Dorigo

Ⓔ

From Venice with Algae

From Venice with Algae is a new generation of stamps made of polluting algae — a project that resulted from designer Pablo Dorigo's search for a product that could ideally convey the story and beauty of Algae Paper®. Born in 1992, Algae Paper® was created when the Italian government commissioned the Venetian paper company Favini to find an innovative way to use the build-up of algae that was harming the ecosystem in the Venitian Lagoon. After much experimenting and dialogues with Favini in the process, Pablo created the stamps to share Algae Paper®'s unique heritage. Instead of using typical but expensive watermarking techniques that typically make counterfeiting difficult, he also came up with the idea to reconsider the design of the codes to make them graphically appealing but still readable by optical sensors. By travelling all over the world, the stamps play a big part in disseminating an important message of sustainability.

Could you please elaborate on your research/development process? How important is it in the overall scheme of things and how do your findings influence the final design work?

In a bid to better understand the algae paper's materiality, I learned how to make the paper from scratch with the raw ingredients required, including thin powdered algae, coarse powdered algae and cellulose fibres. The production of paper was divided into three phases: preparing the pulp into fibres, forming the paper on a wire-mesh mould, and drying and finishing the paper's surface. The first step in the process was to hang the cellulose fibres in clear water for 24 hours, allowing them to macerate. These fibres were then moved into a container and mixed with the thin and coarse powdered algae in different amounts, depending on the desired colour and texture of the final result. A deckle — a frame-like device used to shape the pulp — was then dipped into the container and used to scoop up the fibres, before they were left to dry under a press for 48 hours.

How do you typically work and communicate with your client or overcome differences in opinion to achieve the best results? Following which, what do you hope to inspire/change in audiences from this project?

It's important be inspired by the company you're working with as a first step — to breathe their air, to listen to them. Ultimately, the most important goal is to bring the best products possible into people's lives in terms of efficiency, sustainability, aesthetics and so on. If your intentions are honest, other goals can be achieved, such as the satisfaction of having done something relevant.

How do the skills/abilities of a designer come into play, particularly in projects for the greater good? What have you personally learned/taken away from this project?

The main strength in being a designer for me is the capability of interconnecting different experiences and learnings. This is what we could call a holistic approach. External points of view allow the company to expand their horizons and vice versa. With Favini, I learned a lot about the magical story of paper as a crucial technology for human evolution and culture. I also learned how important communication is as a whole.

There have been rising discussions on designers' roles and responsibilities over the years. What do you think is/are the core values/mentality designers today need to be equipped with in order to foster a better world?

I think a designer's ambition (or approach) is to make something relevant for the people, and to raise the general quality of life. Of course, it is an extremely complex mission that has to take a lot of factors like sustainability, user experience, profit, company ambitions etc. into consideration, but this complexity, this wide spectrum of elements, is what makes design a llittle bit superficial because of the influence of capitalism and market rules. However, at best, design not only results in a good and meaningful product, but also elevates values in society.

Kosuke Takahashi

©
D

Braille Neue

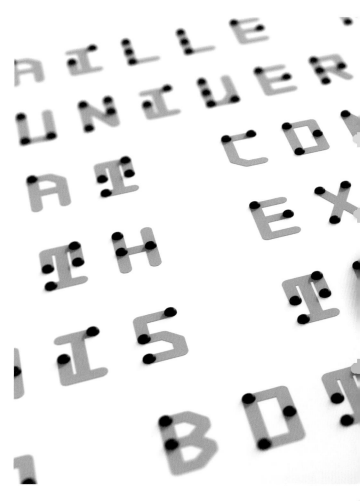

CLIENT
Shibuya City Office,
Panasonic Center Tokyo

Braille Neue is a universal typeface combining Braille with different characters. Product designer
Kosuke Takahashi set out to deliver alternative ways of communication through the sharing of
information between the sighted
and the visually impaired using a
common medium, in addition to
enabling a visual comprehension
of Braille for people who do not
know it. Through the project, he
hoped to help create an inclusive
society, while providing solutions
to common problems such as
missing letters and misprints. To
date, Braille Neue continues to
provide universal support and
and inclusive philosophy for a
variety of facilities, including the
Shibuya City Office and Panasonic Center Tokyo.

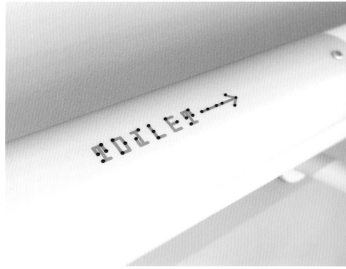

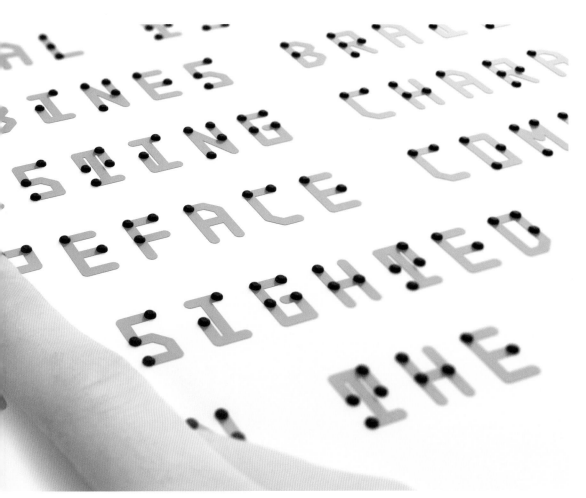

BRAILLE NEUE STANDARD

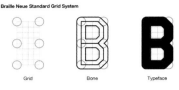

Braille Neue Standard Grid System

Grid   Bone   Typeface

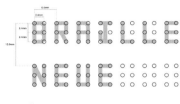

Reference: Braille Rule (conform to Japanese Industrial Standards)

Braille+Character

A B C D E F G H I J K L M N O P Q R S T U V W X Y Z   1 2 3 4 5 6 7 8 9 0

Character

A B C D E F G H I J K L M N O P Q R S T U V W X Y Z   1 2 3 4 5 6 7 8 9 0

Braille

Braille Neue Outline Grid System

Grid   Bone   Typeface

Reference: Braille Rule (conform to Japanese Industrial Standards)

Braille+Character

Character

Braille

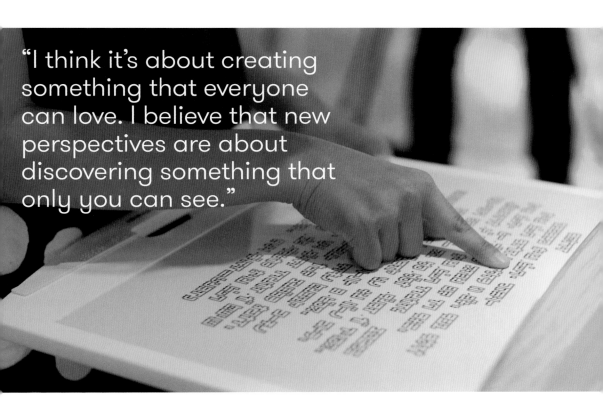

"I think it's about creating something that everyone can love. I believe that new perspectives are about discovering something that only you can see."

Could you please elaborate on your research/development process? How important is it in the overall scheme of things and how do your findings influence the final design work?

Braille Neue was inspired by a visually impaired friend of mine who made me wonder why I couldn't read Braille. I then started designing typefaces with the simple idea of connecting Braille dots with lines. During the development phase, I also noticed that some Braille signage in public spaces were either damaged or indicated completely different meanings. When I asked my friend about it, he said that it has been a common problem, as even though Braille was developed 200 years ago, it is still difficult for sighted people to handle. In 2017, our prototype was used as the logotype for an event, where we came to realise that the typeface was not only making Braille more accessible, but also was sparking conversations between the visually impaired and sighted people.

How do you typically work and communicate with your Client or overcome differences in opinion to achieve the best results? Following which, what do you hope to inspire/change in audiences from this project?

For Braille Neue, the idea of using a common tool to trigger communication between sighted people and the visually impaired was evaluated by the client. If we can empathise with the vision, we can discuss it constructively. I hope that a variety of products will be borne from similar ideas.

How do the skills/abilities of a designer come into play, particularly in projects for the greater good? What have you personally learned/taken away from this project?

Using the power of design, we can embody ideas and materialise them into experience. We can also discover issues that were previously invisible. For Braille Neue, my personal interest in Braille led me to make prototypes and try them out repeatedly, and I was able to discover the invisible problems that exist in society.

KaCaMa Design Lab

ANewToys Library @Tung Tau Estate

CLIENT
ANewToys

As cultural hotbeds that constantly see popular trends come and go across various fields of interest, cities have always had an abundance of preowned toys. Inspired by this unique phenomenon and setting out to alleviate the problem of wastage, ANewToys collaborated with KaCaMa Design Lab to start ANewToys Library, a social project funded by a district council in Hong Kong (China) which sought to promote environmental protection and community resource-sharing through the setting up of a preowned toy rental point/station. Besides organising regular activities and events for children such as librarian training, the project also aimed to promote a sense of civic awareness and social responsibility.

Could you please elaborate on your research/development process? How important is it in the overall scheme of things and how do your findings influence the final design work?

For this project, we planned and developed how the rental point/station would work with our clients as we went through all the details together. It was extremely interesting because we modified the seemingly mundane daily routine of a rental spot operator into a fun, innovative and flexible job. This project demonstrates how constraints make us more creative. We needed to be extra careful in terms of safety because our primary target audience was children, and we needed to keep everything as simple as it could be yet not boring given the space limitations.

How do you typically work and communicate with your client or overcome differences in opinion to achieve the best results? Following which, what do you hope to inspire/change in audiences from this project?

Honest and effective communication was very important in this project, particularly as we needed to develop the design together with our clients instead of simply presenting our ideas. We were forced to choose between a more aesthetic option and a more functional option, and the only way to make a choice was to finalise the priorities with them.

How do the skills/abilities of a designer come into play, particularly in projects for the greater good? What have you personally learned/taken away from this project?

'Form follows function' was definitely the key learning in this project. When it comes to design, sometimes we focus too much on the aesthetics and ignore functionality, which is equally crucial in any kinds of design. In this project, our design had to be able to grow with the toy library, hence, the flexibility and the ability to expand was taken into account in the design process.

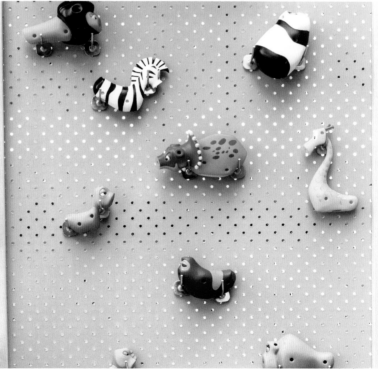

Citron Studio

Ⓔ
Ⓓ

A Better Source

A Better Source is a free and public directory of environmentally conscious resources created for graphic designers and businesses with an emphasis on meeting print, packaging and branding needs. In building the directory collaborating with the creatives involved, creative director of Citron Studio Jennifer James Wright also found that it was important to provide viewers with educational articles to help better inform their sourcing decisions. Today, A Better Source includes easy-to-digest reads on topics such as circular design, the challenges of bioplastics, and real-world examples of responsible design. It also has a Literacy Library which gives readers and interested parties a quick guide to basic terminology, common materials and industry certifications.

Could you please elaborate on your research/development process? How important is it in the overall scheme of things and how do your findings influence the final design work?

Thorough research and education is at the core of A Better Source. Our goal in the studio was to make the directory as practical and useful as possible to those in the design industry. Doing so required a great deal of research to ensure accurate, credible information. As such, the outcome is a labour of love and necessitates ongoing support from a handful of research volunteers.

How do you typically work and communicate with your client or overcome differences in opinion to achieve the best results? Following which, what do you hope to inspire/change in audiences from this project?

We hope to inspire conscious creating among the design community — in other words, designing and manufacturing with our planet in mind. That can take many forms, such as designing with less materials, utilising a less harmful production method, or sourcing for materials that can easily be recycled or composted.

How do the skills/abilities of a designer come into play, particularly in projects for the greater good? What have you personally learned/taken away from this project?

As designers, we are often tasked with creating compelling and eye-catching visuals whether they be via identities, packaging, products or otherwise. In doing so, we play a significant role in promoting consumerism and the excessive consumption of goods. That aspect of our industry may never go away, but we as designers have an incredible opportunity to shift our mindset and practices to at least create more consciously. Doing so requires educating yourself, educating your clients, seeking less harmful production methods, designing with less material usage in mind, and so on.

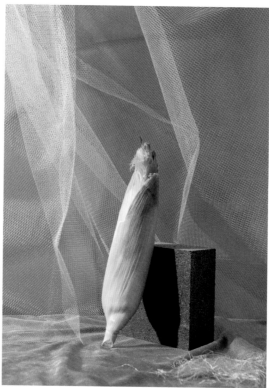

L'Autre Soie

CLIENT
Economic Interest Group (Alynea, Aralis, Est Métropole Habitat, Rhône Saône Habitat, CCO Villeurbanne)

Located within the perimeter of the Carré de Soie district, L'Autre Soie is a project that combines housing reserved for people in difficulty, as well as places dedicated to culture and socio-economic solidarity. It sought to become a creative and attractive place within the city supported by a strong and thriving community, where everyone would be able to find their place in society while contributing to the development of their capacity to act for the whole. The team at Graphéine imagined its visual identity as a manifesto — a powerful statement linking the intangible and the concrete, to bring people together. Designing as a collective, the participative nature of the work allowed the team to question the principle of otherness while promoting a space for free, open and developing expressions.

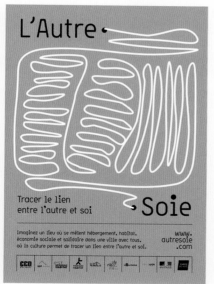

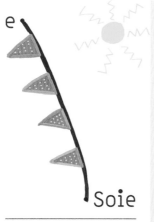

e

Soie

où se mêlent hébergement, habitat,
et solidaire, dans une ville avec tous,
net de tracer un lien entre l'autre et soi.

ou la culture permet de tracer un lien entre l'autre et soi.

«Un ami est
un autre
soi-même.»

Aristote

Thème: Solidarité

L'Autre

rencontres.»

William
Butler Yeats

Thème: Amitié

L'Autre

Tracer le lien
entre l'autre et soi

Soi

Imaginez un lieu où se mêlent hébergement, habitat,
économie sociale et solidaire, dans une ville avec tou
où la culture permet de tracer un lien entre l'autre et s

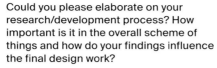

Could you please elaborate on your research/development process? How important is it in the overall scheme of things and how do your findings influence the final design work?

The conceptual phase is extremely important to us, as it is at this stage that we question the subject from all angles. We do not hesitate to mobilise historical, sociological, scientific and artistic knowledge, or any other subject that might shed interesting light on the subject. This is a step towards deepening our knowledge, an essential prerequisite for the emergence of a quality creative response. Within the context of L'Autre Soie, the concept developed completely dictates the form.

How do you typically work and communicate with your client or overcome differences in opinion to achieve the best results? Following which, what do you hope to inspire/change in audiences from this project?

For the L'Autre Soie project, we proposed a very specific approach. As it was fundamentally participatory in nature, we conducted a workshop where the client directly experienced the concept of 'tracing the link between self and other'. We did not come up with any alternative ideas because we believed in the idea proposed. To us, it was a very special project, with a client who was exceptionally open to experimentation.

How do the skills/abilities of a designer come into play, particularly in projects for the greater good? What have you personally learned/taken away from this project?

Initially, the primary objective of design was to put people back at the centre of industrial processes; to make 'edible' what machines produced. Its role was therefore to innovate, translate or facilitate the usage of these products. In this respect, the designer was part of a humanist approach, placing man at the centre of matter. As graphic designers, we create images, signs and messages that will be reproduced ad infinitum, mechanically or electronically. Each image joins other promotional and informational messages that invade our environments. By bringing ideas into the world (and to our clients), we have a part in their success or failure. Today, the indicators are changing, as are the urgencies. Social responsibility is entering the business world. In this respect, designers have a formidable reservoir of resources within them: creativity.

PLASTIC-People Branding

CLIENT
PLASTICPeople

PLASTICPeople upcycles plastic waste to create safe and durable building materials for countless applications around the world. The organisation strives to not only reduce waste and create alternatives to the most common materials on the market, but also empower an entire workforce to make a difference. The PLASTICPeople upcycling model is a reproducable cycle that can be scaled in many ways. Besides naming the brand and designing its visual identity, the team at Rice also sought to create conversations around the relationships that people continue to have with plastic. Elements from the visual identity were used consistently across branded assets to strengthen PLASTICPeople's messaging, including material catalogues, uniforms, and factory facades.

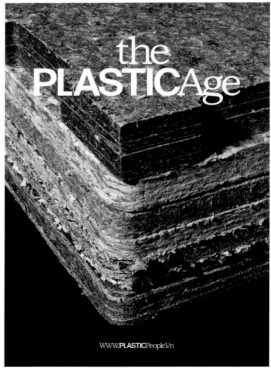

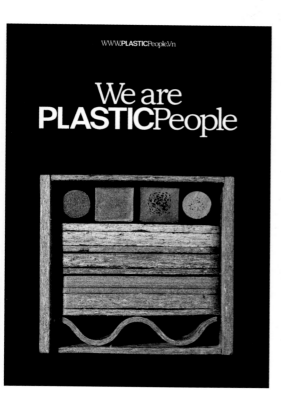

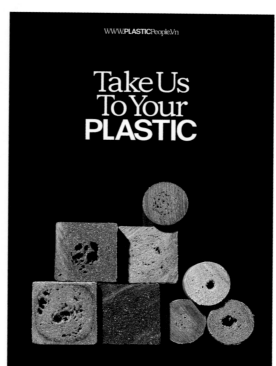

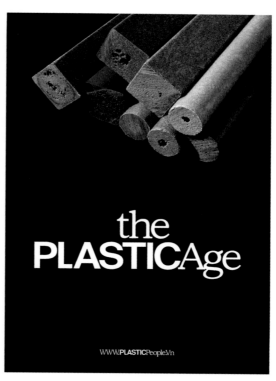

FLOODS AND HURRICANE MOLAVE No. 9 HAVE DESTROYED MANY HOMES IN CENTRAL VIETNAM.

Walls for Central Vietnam

Roots for Central Vietnam!

Could you please elaborate on your research/development process? How important is it in the overall scheme of things and how do your findings influence the final design work?

We always conduct plenty of research. For the PLASTICPeople project, we started by looking at the visual language of plastic itself (even plastic under a microscope), but our journey eventually led to activism and the hippie revolution, including John Lennon's 'Power to the People', which inspired a rich territory for design and language inspiration. Meanderings are good, as they help connections form and can ultimately lead to unexpected solutions.

How do you typically work and communicate with your client or overcome differences in opinion to achieve the best results? Following which, what do you hope to inspire/change in audiences from this project?

There was a point in the PLASTICPeople project where things were very touch-and-go. I was convinced that the name was everything, as people's relationships and responsibilities towards plastic would have to come to mind the moment they heard the name. I knew the clients understood this, but I didn't know if they would have the same enthusiasm about using their name as a hook. We created a long and inspiring narrative to back our naming presentation, but when they loved it, I knew we would have no problem getting the visual identity done and approved.

How do the skills/abilities of a designer come into play, particularly in projects for the greater good? What have you personally learned/taken away from this project?

PLASTICPeople works to change the environment and society while speaking of hope, but it is also a simple materials company. All of this is either hard to grasp, or potentially boring. We had to deliver something that was catchy, fun and simple, but also intellectual. This brand strikes the balance that we love between pop and edge in a thought-provoking way. It would have been easy to to make plastic the enemy most of us see, but we made it the hero instead.

There have been rising discussions on designers' roles and responsibilities over the years. What do you think is/are the core values/mentality designers today need to be equipped with in order to foster a better world?

Designers are key stakeholders in the projects they design for. To design well, one must know the project inside out, including the implications of 'helping' whatever the 'cause' is. We all know the power of design. It can often be a make or break factor for an organisation or product seeking to connect with people. Designers have the power to put themselves and their passions towards projects that align with their values. This has always been the responsibility of the designer as the visionary of the future. Propel the meaningful — or do not.

Extract

In 2017, G.F Smith launched
Extract, a pioneering new paper
that tackles the global problem of
disposable coffee cups lined with
plastic. The paper itself is the
result of a unique process and
collaboration between consumer,
recycler and papermaker —
a dynamic combination of
chemistry and artistry that takes
disposable cups and transforms
them into beautiful paper,
which is available in 10 colours
all inspired and drawn directly
from nature. Through Extract,
G.F Smith set out to inspire a
better awareness of waste and its
impact on the environment. For
the launch of the paper, the team
worked with its ongoing design
partner, Made Thought to create
a unique installation that made
a lasting impression.

We use 4,861 paper cups every minute in the UK. That's 7 million a day. Or just over 2.5 billion a year.

Less than 1 in 400 of these cups gets recycled. The rest go to landfill or incineration.

From cup, to

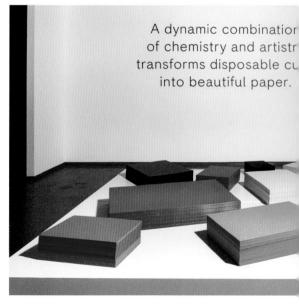

A dynamic combination of chemistry and artistry transforms disposable cups into beautiful paper.

r.

Could you please elaborate on your research/development process? How important is it in the overall scheme of things and how do your findings influence the final design work?

Coffee on the go is more popular than ever: about 7m paper cups of it are consumed every day in the UK. Yet less than 1 in 400 of those cups gets recycled. It's partly chemistry – the polyethylene that stops the cup getting soggy makes recycling difficult, and it takes a special process to separate the plastic from other paper waste, which makes it expensive. That's why G.F Smith partnered with CupCycling™ by James Cropper to offer a solution by design. With the technology, we're taking 90% of the waste from each cup and converting it back into FSC certified paper fibre. This means every sheet of Extract in 380gsm paper contains at least five upcycled coffee cups. The remaining 10% of waste will become something else entirely. Because it's a zero waste process, the more Extract that gets used, the fewer cups go to landfill or incineration.

How do you typically work and communicate with your client or overcome differences in opinion to achieve the best results? Following which, what do you hope to inspire/change in audiences from this project?

Recycling is just the start of reducing waste. Through our Extract Sheet Policy, paper can be bought to the nearest single digit (as long as the order is more than 25 sheets), so only the amount needed is ordered, minimising paper waste. Extract has also been developed to work exceptionally well with the latest digital printing technology, so only the amount needed is printed, minimising ink waste. Upcycling addresses the problem, not the cause – so the creation of this exceptional FSC-certified paper is just a start to reduce plastic consumption and the impact it has on our environment. Changes in our methods of production and day-to-day operations, including the installation of solar panels at our factory, are also helping us to reduce our carbon footprint.

How do the skills/abilities of a designer come into play, particularly in projects for the greater good? What have you personally learned/taken away from this project?

Waste is everywhere, so what are we going to do about it? We know the problem, but where are the solutions? Waste is an increasing serious issue that affects all of us, but some brands are thinking differently about its creative re-use and how we can create thoughtful, progressive products whilst reducing its impact. Extract shows us how we can transform the way we think about waste and how innovation, behaviour and creativity are at the heart of this change. In our continuing drive to be more innovative, pioneering and disruptive as a brand, G.F Smith remains committed to sustainability. We aim to continually challenge ourselves but above all challenge the global paper industry.

There have been rising discussions on designers' roles and responsibilities over the years. What do you think is/are the core values/mentality designers today need to be equipped with in order to foster a better world?

Designers have a responsibility and duty, specifically in terms of product design, to consider the product lifecycle, the environmental impact of that, and how a product can be repurposed at the end of its life. The takeaway coffee cup is an example of that where, yes, of course, there is form and function in terms of design. It works, it's convenient, it has purpose, but at no point was there consideration for how that product could be disposed of or reused. Plastic laminated to paper is one of the most difficult materials to deconstruct, hence up until the technology developed for Extract, coffee cups had one route at the end of their lives: the landfill. Consumers today want better products and better design thinking.

reMarkable

CLIENT
reMarkable

Working in close collaboration with the team at reMarkable, Goods' packaging work for the former's recently-launched device is a perfect example of stylish and sustainble design. Described as the world's thinnest tablet or digital notebook at only 4.7mm, the paper-like device sets out to replace printed documents. Inspired by its specs, the product's packaging was used as a 'canvas' to emboss its silhouette upon at a 1:1 scale for a tangible and tactile experience. All the packaging materials used are recyclable worldwide and, instead of industry-standard plastic film, the tablet comes on a custom-moulded pulp tray — wrapped in bespoke, die-cut translucent paper. What's more, the new packaging is half the size of the previous version, which not only reduces material use and production costs, but also doubles shipping density.

"We started Goods as a packaging design studio focusing on ethics, not just aesthetics. Curiosity and a focused mind is all you need to create the future."

Could you please elaborate on your research/development process? How important is it in the overall scheme of things and how do your findings influence the final design work?

The reMarkable no-plastic-concept was inspired by the analogue world, from the world of books and libraries to printed matter.

How do you typically work and communicate with your client or overcome differences in opinion to achieve the best results? Following which, what do you hope to inspire/change in audiences from this project?

We worked closely with the in-house design team at reMarkable in a bid to remove all plastic from the product packaging, so as to inspire the rest of the tech world to package their goods more sustainably.

How do the skills/abilities of a designer come into play, particularly in projects for the greater good? What have you personally learned/taken away from this project?

Working with the reMarkable in-house team, we had all kinds of skill sets available at our disposal, which was really helpful in our efforts. Completing a global, bespoke packaging project with budget limitations was really demanding, but so worth it because we got to produce a new innovation by using only paper as packaging for the tablet.

Moby Digg

E
S

Meltdown Flags

CLIENTS
METER Group, Serviceplan Group

Glaciers are a source of life. Besides holding 69% of our planet's freshwater, providing millions of people around the world with drinking water, they are also important for power and irrigation. Scientists have warned that if global warming does not stop by 2050, glaciers will be gone forever. Meltdown Flags is a climate data initiative that visualises the retreat of glaciers by reducing the amount of white in country flags, in making people aware and helping them understand the long-term consequences of global warming. The team at Moby Digg also designed a website and an interactive exhibition providing more information, where visitors could visualise the degree of glacier retreat by country and access relevant data.

2020

2050

2050

MELTDOWNFLAGS.ORG

MEL

1995

1995

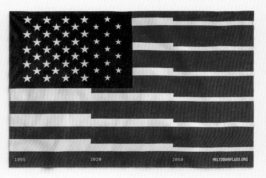

Could you please elaborate on your research/development process? How important is it in the overall scheme of things and how do your findings influence the final design work?

I would say research and development are an inherent part of the design process in our studio, no matter what the project is. It all starts with the team really understanding the subject matter at hand, as well as the client we are working together with. Part of this research is also experimentation. Often, from researching specific data and tools to process data, we can find an aesthetic which we think is interesting and hopefully innovative as well. We are often looking for ways with which we can translate information into something easily digestible by using visual tools; graphics, shapes, colours. In other words, we work on translating the rather abstract into something visually appealing and understandable.

How do you typically work and communicate with your client or overcome differences in opinion to achieve the best results? Following which, what do you hope to inspire/change in audiences from this project?

The Moby Digg team functions as a group of close friends, which makes communication between us natural and something we value a lot. This is an approach that we also take to our clients. Not that we force them to be our friends or anything! We just like to have a personal connection with the people we surround ourselves with. That way, differences in opinion don't have to be a big issue. When you get to know each other, you can understand where somebody else is coming from and why they might think differently about something. In this project, we put extra focus on the major consequences of climate change — the melting of glaciers. We hope that the data visualisations make people think more about how climate change in one location can also affect different parts of our world. At the end of the day, we are all in this together.

How do the skills/abilities of a designer come into play, particularly in projects for the greater good? What have you personally learned/taken away from this project?

A designer visualises information. The choices one makes in this visualisation are highly important. Colours, symbols, text — they all carry meaning, and when a designer is not aware of how their choices can affect the information presented, it becomes a big problem. As a designer, there is a great possibility to contribute to the greater good by sharing knowledge and information with many people. This makes it necessary for them to choose what and how to share. At the studio, we aim to put our competences to good use. Through this project, we really felt inspired to shed extra light on climate change-related issues with as many people as possible.

"At Moby Digg, we strongly believe in having personal relationships with people and sharing stories and experiences. As designers today, we think it is very important to gain knowledge from as many different voices as possible. This creates empathy, which we think should be at the core of all creative jobs."

Festival Simbiòtic

CLIENT
WE ACT

We Act is a non-profit cultural association created with the aim of promoting and normalising the participation of people with disabilities in the performing arts as spectators, creators and producers. Its work focuses on the elimination of physical and communicative barriers in theatres by promoting the use of accessibility measures to generate new exhibition spaces and accessible stage training. For Festival Simbiòtic, its first accessible scenic arts festival in Barcelona in 2019, the team at Pràctica and Guillem Casasus were inspired by the event's unyielding spirit on social rights to use hard-hitting and compelling images and copy to make the problems of disabled persons more visible and create meaningful visual impact.

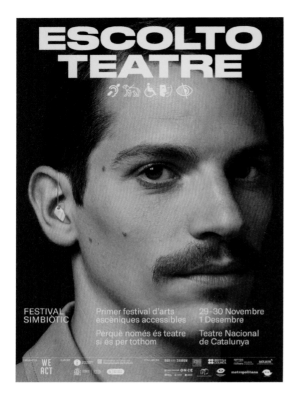

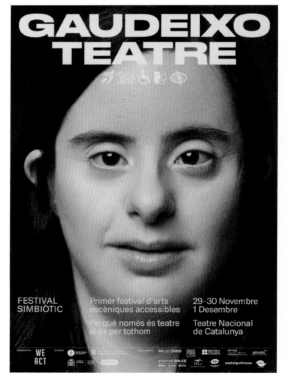

"As communicators, we must be aware of what is being divulged: we cannot just become hands that execute and give shape to any message without asking ourselves what it is saying. We need to be responsible for the stories we tell."

Could you please elaborate on your research/development process? How important is it in the overall scheme of things and how do your findings influence the final design work?

Research is key to developing any project properly. Every client comes from a completely different background, so it is fundamental to study the context, understand their communication needs and detect what is key for the project. From this study, the idea that will frame all the design decisions will arise, including the project's final appearance. Following this course is what gives us our style, and how we offer tailor-made solutions to our clients.

How do you typically work and communicate with your client or overcome differences in opinion to achieve the best results? Following which, what do you hope to inspire/change in audiences from this project?

Conversation is our communication mode with clients. Great work comes from good relationships based on trust, which can only be generated from dialogue and respect.

Festival Simbiotic set out to open theatre doors to diversity, breaking free from communication barriers encountered by the disabled. The campaign offers audiences a glimpse of the hard realities they face and gives visibility to their problems.

How do the skills/abilities of a designer come into play, particularly in projects for the greater good? What have you personally learned/taken away from this project?

We are always excited to work with ethical and sustainable entities. Design has the power to create positive change and we strive to contribute to this transformation through our creativity.

The Nest Project

The Nest Project by Fieldwork Facility is a citizen-led project aimed at nurturing bird life in inner-city areas, where people in the community play a part in encouraging birds to nest in their own neighbourhoods. Nests start their life in the home, school or office, where project participants are encouraged to prepare the nest for birds by using a pencil for a week. The nest's 'dowel' is actually a pencil and sharpener, where each time a pencil is sharpened, you are making more of a home for the incoming birds. Designed to exist in the urban environment by easily attaching onto existing lamp-posts and street furniture, the nests do not only serve as homes for birds but also urban interventions that highlight nature's place in our urban fabric.

Mon – Fri
8.30 am – 6.30 pm

@fieldworkfcltynest

📍 Bishopsgate. Lamppost 4. London #EC2M

Tweet, tweet! Recent activity at 14:00, 03/04/15

Could you please elaborate on your research/development process? How important is it in the overall scheme of things and how do your findings influence the final design work?

As a designer, I'm incredibly invested in cities, public spaces and placemaking, and whilst I'm at home in the city, I actually grew up in the countryside and have started to miss some of the elements that aren't as prevalent in cities; elements that I believe make neighbourhoods nicer places to live and work. Whilst at the Royal College of Art, I had this throwaway idea: a pencil sharpener fashioned as a birdhouse, it sat on my desk, it was fun but didn't feel right as a product — so I put it on the shelf and forgot about it. Fast forward to a few years of living in London and reading about bird and bee populations in cities, I wanted to do something to help. I realised that this little bird-house-pencil-sharpener idea could be reverse engineered. Instead of it being just a product to sharpen pencils, it could be a medium to engage people in helping build a real nest for real birds in their own neighbourhoods.

How do you typically work and communicate with your Client or overcome differences in opinion to achieve the best results? Following which, what do you hope to inspire/change in audiences from this project?

My favourite element of this project was that the nest had two roles. On one hand, they were homes for birds, and on the other hand, they were brightly coloured urban interventions for humans, highlighting our proximity to nature and how we can live alongside each other in cities.

How do the skills/abilities of a designer come into play, particularly in projects for the greater good? What have you personally learned/taken away from this project?

If I were to ask most designers 'what does a designer do?', I'm pretty confident the common answer would be to say that designers are problem solvers. I think a large part of what we do is problem-solving *but* here's the thing – what if problem-solving was only 75% of what a designer

could do? What would you do with that other 25% of your time? I'm an idealist but I really think that design is such an amazing platform to do so so much more, whether as entrepreneurs, broadcasters or community leaders. We've got skillsets to do so much good and bring people together and connect dots.

There have been rising discussions on designers' roles and responsibilities over the years. What do you think is/are the core values/mentality designers today need to be equipped with in order to foster a better world?

If I were to look out my window right now, I would see a few pigeons but not a lot of other bird species – but actually, cities across the world are home to 20% of the world's bird species. What if all you had to do to encourage more birdlife in your neighbourhood was to work in pencil for one week? The nests start their life in the school, home or office. Inside the nest is a little pencil sharpener and all you have to do is to sharpen your pencil for a week to create a cosy home for a bird inside. The reality is birds can be pretty fussy. If they don't like the pencil shavings inside their nests, they will just kick them out...but that's not really the point! The point is we are trying to get people to become more engaged and involved in creating homes for birds in their own neighbourhoods.

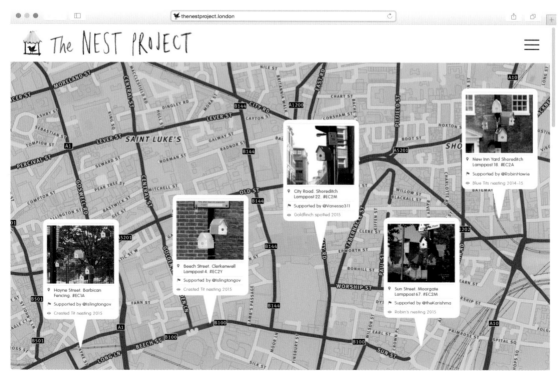

KaCaMa Design Lab   ©

Mody Road Garden

CLIENT
Art Promotion Office

Public spaces are a precious resource to all densely-packed metropolitan cities, with most of them owned/managed by the government. To spark public imagination on the use of public spaces, the team at KaCaMa Design Lab designed a series of furniture for people to interact with, on top of organising community events around them. Created as a new form of community engagement, Mody Road Garden presented colourful, geometric furniture as platforms with different heights for multiple uses, including but not limited to rest areas, event backdrops and social interaction sites. Accessories could even be added to the furniture's perforated stainless steel surfaces to transform them into different shapes and facilitate different outcomes. By engaging the public in participation and planning, the garden also built up the people's sense of belonging.

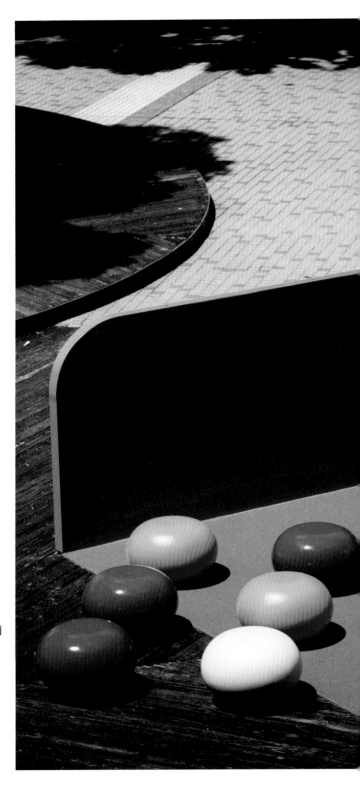

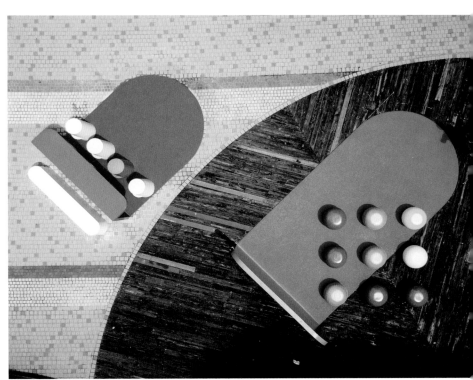

Could you please elaborate on your research/development process? How important is it in the overall scheme of things and how do your findings influence the final design work?

Through extensive observation in the early stages of the project, we learned that the tranquil and beautiful Mody Road Garden was extremely underused. It is geographically isolated, far from the main street or any residential area, and surrounded by Grade-B office buildings. A unique quality about this space is its proximity to art and cultural spaces. We reckoned that this could be the highlight of the project; to seamlessly blend art and culture into the environmental and product design. We believe creative, comfortable seating and functional installations could encourage public interaction and increase connectivity.

How do you typically work and communicate with your client or overcome differences in opinion to achieve the best results? Following which, what do you hope to inspire/change in audiences from this project?

We believe that helping our clients to visualise the final outcome is key to achieving the best results in most projects. In our experience, if budget is not the main factor, the reason our clients disagree with our opinion is usually because they find it difficult to picture the result, or the goal of the project was not clearly articulated. Designers solve problems with creativity, and we make full use of that when it comes to understanding and communicating with our clients because they have a problem to solve. In this project, we hope that our solutions stimulate creativity, not only for the users but most importantly, our clients. Everyone is a stakeholder of the public space — ultimately, it is always the interactions and human touch that give a city/space its personality.

How do the skills/abilities of a designer come into play, particularly in projects for the greater good? What have you personally learned/taken away from this project?

We believe that designers are observant, creative, and relatively good at improvising. These abilities enable us to understand a problem thoroughly through as many perspectives as possible. It is important not to overlook anything that looks unimportant on the surface, particularly in projects for the greater good. A small modification could make a huge difference. We learned that staying humble and curious can take your design to the next level. Inspiration might come from a tree, an old lady taking a stroll in the park, a bird that nests on the lamp, etc. Our design is only a tool/hardware to reactivate a space, and sustaining public engagement is the most important part.

What's Your Proposition?

CLIENT

Plymouth College of Art

In 2018, the Plymouth College of Art (PCA) revealed its 10-year strategy, which was underlined by its manifesto based on social justice and creative learning. In helping it produce a radical campaign intended to change creative education policy at a governmental level, the team at TEMPLO started their creative process by embracing the college's strategic plan, centering their work around the call to action and final point in PCA's manifesto, 'What's Your Proposition?'. Using digital graffiti made of the words 'social justice' and 'creative learning', they captured authentic, hand-drawn responses to the question from students, matching them to their imagery on communication materials.

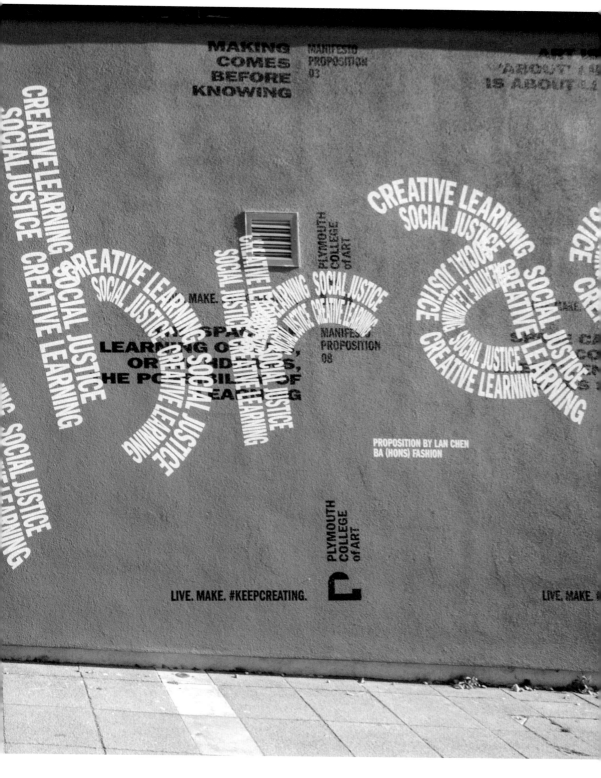

Could you please elaborate on your research/development process? How important is it in the overall scheme of things and how do your findings influence the final design work?

Working alongside the Principal of PCA Andrew Brewerton, we were able to gain an insight into the 10- to 15-year strategy for the College, which had creative learning and social justice in its DNA. It was only through getting under the skin of PCA's unique pedagogy that we were able to arrive at the creative solution.

How do you typically work and communicate with your client or overcome differences in opinion to achieve the best results? Following which, what do you hope to inspire/change in audiences from this project?

This project was caught in the crossfire between the commercial need to fill spaces in the college while also raising awareness of PCA's unique ethos. The way we resolved this was to make the campaign open source, and invite current and potential students to share their propositions with the world while being a part of the campaign itself. This approach

mental health matters Revolt!  EMPOWER COMMUNITY

EMBRACE MISTAKES

The future is female

Dance like no one's watching

KINDNESS PREVAILS

Be you

destroy the patriarchy not the planet

MAKE ART

PROTECT YOUR OCEANS

BREATHE

SINK OR SWIM

rewild yourself

Just Your movement

fight like a girl

MAKING IS AS IMPORTANT AS READING AND WRITING, AS SCIENCE & MATHS

MANIFESTO PROPOSITION

MAKING COMES BEFORE KNOWING

MANIFESTO PROPOSITION

ART IS NOT 'ABOUT' LIFE, IT IS ABOUT LIVING

MANIFESTO PROPOSITION

THE PURPOSE OF LEARNING IS INSEPARABLE FROM THAT OF LIVING YOUR LIFE

MANIFESTO PROPOSITION

EDUCA LEAR NO 'SU HIDE

PLYMOUTH COLLEGE of ART

WHAT'S YOUR PROPOSITION?

CREATIVE LEARNING SOCIAL JUSTICE

PROTEST

CREATIVE LEARNING SOCIAL JUSTICE

MANIFESTO PROPOSITION 10

Share

LIVE. MAKE. #KEEPCREATING.

was pretty ahead of its time and one of the first times that a college stuck their neck out, was uncensored, and tied their ethos to their brand in this way. Ultimately, the campaign was designed to recruit the right type of student; those who have agency to affect social change.

How do the skills/abilities of a designer come into play, particularly in projects for the greater good? What have you personally learned/taken away from this project?

This project was one of those instances where the client was right. We did not initially think it was possible to combine so many elements in the campaign, but the client insisted and ultimately made the final outcome better.

Gambling Risks Campaign

CLIENT
Madrid City Council

Gambling has always been a difficult topic to talk about with a broad target audience, whether it be with teenagers or adults. In addressing the issue, Familia's campaign focused on three different goals: to raise awareness on the real dangers of gambling, to alert people on the usual deceptions in the advertising of betting companies, as well as to communicate the role of the Institute of Addictions of Madrid in providing support services. The concept of the campaign was based on the dichotomy of idealisation versus reality, with visuals translating these two worlds complemented by compelling copy. Through the concise, direct, contemporary and synthetic campaign, the team avoided unnecessary formal excess.

Could you please elaborate on your research/development process? How important is it in the overall scheme of things and how do your findings influence the final design work?

Our work process is made up of several phases. The first is to understand the issue to be solved or the communication objective of the project. The second is to know what type of solution is optimal to resolve the issue or the contents of the message that should be communicated, especially in the campaign. Finally, the third phase is to visually translate the message to be communicated. We believe that following these three phases in their correct order is vital to creating functional projects, not just formal ones.

How do you typically work and communicate with your client or overcome differences in opinion to achieve the best results? Following which, what do you hope to inspire/change in audiences from this project?

We start from the idea that you have to listen before speaking. Never go into a meeting with preconceptions. Our job is to listen, ask questions, and then translate those ideas into graphic images, and above all, have the ability to create projects where the client and the public feel represented.

How do the skills/abilities of a designer come into play, particularly in projects for the greater good? What have you personally learned/taken away from this project?

Beyond technical and aesthetic knowledge, the skills that allow us to reach a social or common benefit are transversal capacities in everyone. First of all, and above all, I think that in order to create projects that add value to society, we must train ourselves to have empathy and try to get away from our closed points of view. We need to try to zoom out and be as objective as possible, within our own subjectivities.

There have been rising discussions on designers' roles and responsibilities over the years. What do you think is/are the core values/mentality designers today need to be equipped with in order to foster a better world?

I would highlight honesty before any other value. To communicate and design, we must be honest with ourselves and with others. We must work thinking that the discourse we defend is the best from a general point of view, not ours (portfolio, social network). If we think that the proposal is really the best proposal for the client or user, we will be doing a good job, or at least, it will be the best result that we can offer at that specific moment.

emograms with LOVE

CLIENT
Chongqing and Lotte Gallery Exhibition

'emograms with LOVE' was an international solo exhibition by kissmiklos at the Lotte Gallery, Incheon in 2020. The exhibition consisted of two parts: the first being a space built around emograms and the Ball.Room installation, with the second revolving around a new installation called the LOVE Field and a typography-based sculpture. Artist kissmiklos was inspired by the fact that emoji, the Japanese word for 'picture'+'letter/character', was included in the Oxford Dictionaries in 2015. He sought to put 'lost words' back into the drawings and pictograms that have been taking over our lives on mobile phones and computers today. Besides paying homage to Harvey R. Ball, who drew the first smiley, and eliciting smiles, the exhibits also set out to prompt viewers into examining how human digital communication can be.

Could you please elaborate on your research/development process? How important is it in the overall scheme of things and how do your findings influence the final design work?

I typically do my research before starting a new project — and it definitely affects the final result. In 2015, I read an article stating that Oxford Dictionaries had chosen 'emoji' as the word of the year. I found this very interesting and did my research from there. We started written communication using drawings and pictograms, and then we began simplfying these to letters and characters. After the birth of mobile and computer communication, we went the other way round, recreating drawings and pictograms from these letters and characters, incorporating them into our daily lives. Through 'emograms', I sought to put the lost words back into emojis.

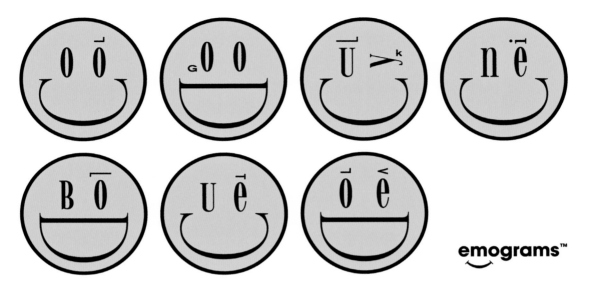

emograms™

"It is important to be as informed and sensitive about what happens in our world as possible."

How do you typically work and communicate with your client or overcome differences in opinion to achieve the best results? Following which, what do you hope to inspire/change in audiences from this project?

There is a concept behind all of my work and I always insist on it. I'm open to new ideas and changes from a client if it makes sense. While the client would have a strong reason as to why these changes are necessary, I'm always fighting against ideas that do not fit with the concept. Fortunately, those who want to work with me usually trust in my abilities and experience. I hope to inspire audiences with my work and make people feel better.

How do the skills/abilities of a designer come into play, particularly in projects for the greater good? What have you personally learned/taken away from this project?

A good designer has the skill to create memorable projects that affect people and ensure that every part of the project is interconnected. Every new exhibition is a new experience for me, and I try to put this knowledge to the next show to give back a bigger and better experience to audiences.

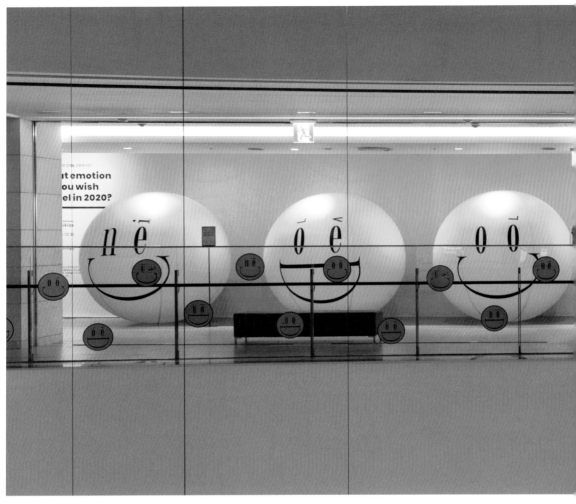

Supertrash

CLIENT
Supertrash

Supertrash is a small, family-run collection service with a big purpose: to help divert as much waste as possible from landfills. In designing its new brand identity, the team at Seachange were aware that a rubbish truck livery was required to make use of the biggest, most visible canvas. Using a small fleet of five trucks, it set out to make some noise and created something that could not be ignored — a bold, fluoro-pink, comic-inspired pattern that took over the trucks, as a nod to the loud bangs and crashing sounds typically associated with them. Ultimately, the reimagined rubbish trucks celebrated their inherent functionality in a colourful way, hugely increasing Supertrash's profiles.

Could you please elaborate on your research/development process? How important is it in the overall scheme of things and how do your findings influence the final design work?

Research plays an integral role in our process — once the brief is established, we launch into this phase. It firstly involves deep-diving into the sector that the company operates in. For us, it's super important to understand the industry, what's been done and what hasn't. From the brief, we would have identified key themes which we then loosely research. We often look to the past for inspiration, or other unexpected places over trendy design blogs.

Supertrash operates in the waste management industry, which is an industry that hasn't really had any design love, so we wanted to give it a real nudge and create a category-breaking brand. It is very passionate about sustainability and clever initiatives to reduce waste, so we looked into activism vernacular to give them a voice. To tie the visual identity to their name, we looked into pop-art and comic-inspired graphics, as well as more contemporary reference points like rad Nike posters which capture energy and dynamism.

How do you typically work and communicate with your client or overcome differences in opinion to achieve the best results? Following which, what do you hope to inspire/change in audiences from this project?

We work very closely with our clients to firstly establish the brief and strategic direction. These stages help to form trust, which you have to have if you want to challenge the client with your work. We were lucky with Supertrash in that the client was very brave and let us go for it. We generally find that issues typically arise when there is a lack of communication, and the simplest way to solve that is to chat it through, whether in-person, on Zoom or via a quick phone call. Supertrash was a very important project for us, as we really believe in their work. We wanted to give them a voice, and make people stop and take notice of what they do to help our planet.

How do the skills/abilities of a designer come into play, particularly in projects for the greater good? What have you personally learned/taken away from this project?

As designers, we strive to find the perfect balance between being strategic and playful. You have to know who you're talking to and what action you want to inspire. For Supertrash, it was all about awareness. Public good projects need to be super accessible, but because there's so much work already being done in the sector and everyone's competing for your attention, it needs to stand out and be memorable in order to be successful. It doesn't matter what sector you are creating work for — what's much more important is having a passionate and brave client that has a vision, and something they want to say. Most designers would probably turn their nose up at doing a brand for a waste management company, but for us, it was very exciting and gave us the opportunity to create something category breaking.

SuperShe

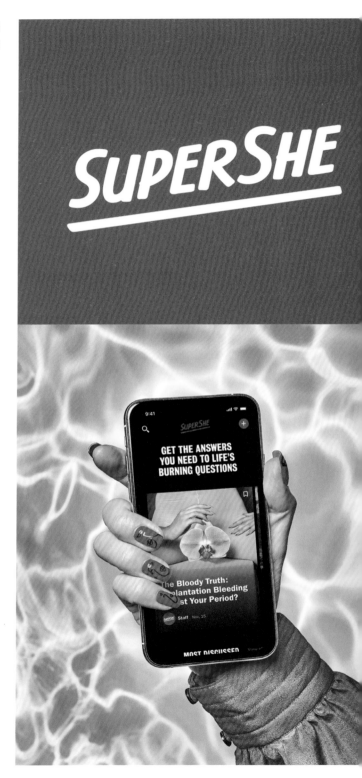

CLIENT
SuperShe

Tucked away in the Baltic Sea and located off the coast of Finland, SuperShe started as a women's only private island — a place where women could not only be themselves away from the distractions of the outside world, but also form bonds and lift each other up. As the interest in SuperShe grew for those wanting a sense of community, founder Kristina Roth eventually realised that a private island was inaccessible to many — which is why she decided to bring the experience onto an app. The team at &Walsh created the branding, strategy and merchandise for the brand, inspired by protest posters of women's marches throughout history and driven by the need to create honest communication in a market saturated with fluff.

SUPER BOSS

OR SUPER CHILL

SUPER
CHILLED
VODKA

When life gives you problems,
distill them into vodka.

SuperShe

40% ALC./VOL. (80 PROOF) 1 LITER

NO
FLUFF
SOAP

THIS SOAP WILL NOT GIVE
YOU SUPERPOWERS, MAKE
SOMEONE FALL IN LOVE
WITH YOU, OR WASH AWAY
MEMORIES OF YOUR BAD EX.
THIS IS JUST A GOOD OLD
QUALITY BODY BAR FOR
WOMEN THAT KNOW BETTER.

SuperShe

SUPER BLAAH

SuperShe

SUPER PUMPED

Ken Lo

More Hugs Less Hate

Borne out of a deep-rooted desire to better the world through design, More Hugs Less Hate is the latest initiative to spring from the mind of designer Ken Lo of leading creative agency BLOW. Drawing from a wide-ranging plethora of elements from contemporary pop culture, the project combines his signature bold and flat style with distinctive iconography to create a graphic design series that speaks to the heart. With its universally relatable message of love, it aims to instil change in public perceptions through its refreshing earnestness, on top of being a meditative reflection of Ken's personal history and unique view on the world.

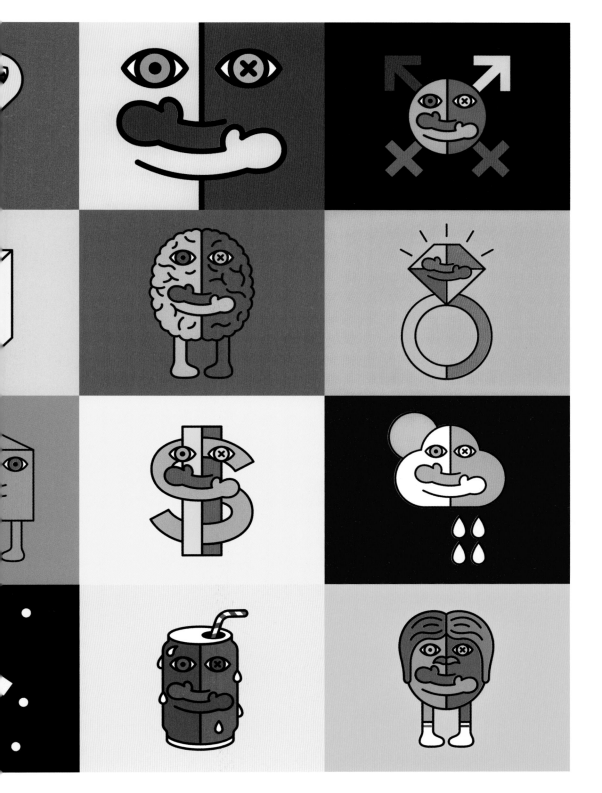

Could you please elaborate on your research/development process? How important is it in the overall scheme of things and how do your findings influence the final design work?

Most of my work is client-commissioned, so I wanted to try something self-initiated and honest to myself without any strategy. I began to work with bold graphics since I found icons like punctuation signs easy to understand and straight-forward for the public, engaging with communities in a more long lasting relationship. The icon for hugging indicates the meaning of coexistence. It represents both the physical and mental sides in an abstract way, bringing contradictory elements together, e.g., right (rational) and left (emotional) brain.

During the process, the 911 incident occurred and inspired my work. I hoped I could make people focus more on positive thinking, hence the idea of 'more hugs, less hate'. There wasn't really a plan at the beginning. I only wanted to do something happy and positive, so it's more of an archive for my personal development.

How do you typically work and communicate with your client or overcome differences in opinion to achieve the best results? Following which, what do you hope to inspire/change in audiences from this project?

Commercial projects are more of a collaboration with your clients, where you have to work with their ideas and take them into consideration whether good or bad. I think the biggest difference between working for a client or for yourself is the initiation of the project, who makes the brief and sets the direction, and most importantly the aims and goals of the project.

To get the best results, you must take criticism seriously and face it. Explore, think and try more, especially why you want to be a graphic designer, and what you can do to make an impact.

For this project, I hope to tell everyone that we should do something like call for action and educate each other, as that's the step we should all take that adds value to the project.

How do the skills/abilities of a designer come into play, particularly in projects for the greater good? What have you personally learned/taken away from this project?

Design has the power to connect people with each other, and it isn't limited to geographical limitations or existing clients. As a world language, we find similarities in values through design and build relationships with people outside of our existing clients.

Through my projects, I've learned that instead of waiting for people to do something positive, you should do it yourself – then inspire others to take action too.

There have been rising discussions on designers' roles and responsibilities over the years. What do you think is/are the core values/mentality designers today need to be equipped with in order to foster a better world?

1. Be honest with yourself. As a designer, don't just show off your techniques and skills. Don't just pretend to be cool or act cool. You have to face your inner self and be true to yourself. Techniques and skills are only for the short term, not for your whole life.

2. Think — how can society benefit from this?

3. Know who you are; and what your skills and power are to make yourself and others happy.

TED
Countdown

CLIENTS
Chris Anderson, Mike Femia,
Logan McClure Davda

&Walsh developed the branding
and campaign for TED's Countdown event and initiative which
set out to halve emissions in 10
years. With a globally streamed
launch in October 2020, the
summit's mission was to bring the
greatest thinkers from all over the
world together to work towards
a single goal — to turn the tide
on climate change. Inspired by
a flip clock to create a sense of
urgency around how little time
humanity has left to change climate change and prevent mass
extinction, the design team at
&Walsh used the shock value of
an organisation like TED saying
powerful lines such as 'we give
up' in the marketing campaign.

WHAT ARE YOU GOING TO DO TO JOIN THE COUNTDOWN?

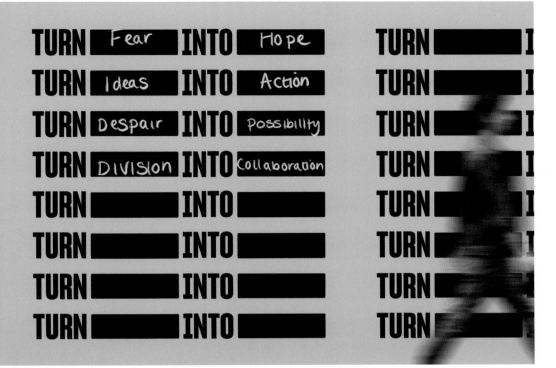

Could you please elaborate on your research/development process? How important is it in the overall scheme of things and how do your findings influence the final design work?

The purpose of this project was to launch TED's initiative to halve emissions in 10 years and turn the tide on climate change. The event and ongoing campaign strove to not only bring together activists and scientists from around the world, but to also unify everyday people and educate them on what they can do to help. The target audience included every single person on the planet because it's everyone's responsibility to be earth-conscious and aware of the changing world around them. People are used to drowning out climate warnings, so we wanted to find a way that would actually grab their attention and get them to listen. We did this through the flip clock, which creates a sense of urgency, and bold/shocking messages that are impossible to ignore. Once we had people's attention, the goal was to inspire people to help create change through TED's action-based plans and initiatives.

How do the skills/abilities of a designer come into play, particularly in projects for the greater good? What have you personally learned/taken away from this project?

At &Walsh, we love helping our clients with strategy and messaging in addition to visual/branding. That was my favourite part of this project. We helped with the strategy to go beyond ideas and towards action. This was an important decision, as TED's mission is to 'Spread Ideas'. Everything you see in the copywriting and messaging throughout the brand is centered around igniting action. A lot of hard work went into the project, but it always feels easier when you're passionate about something — and our team cares greatly about the climate crisis. I always tell designers starting off that you have to hone in on the causes you are most passionate about and/or focus on what you want to change in the world. Working on TED Countdown was one of those projects that allowed my team and I to use our creative skills to make a difference.

Anjela Freyja

Be on the Right Side of History

Be on the Right Side of History was born for the Women's March in 2017, when millions of people around the world stood up for equal rights and demanded change from their governments. To commemorate the moment, graphic designer Anjela Freyja created 21 posters, all inspired by first-wave, second-wave, and third-wave feminists, featuring messages that draw attention to the fight for women's rights. All posters were completely free to download and use, and available in a variety of sizes with a photo or as just text, spreading the message of strength in solidarity and calling for people to stand up for what's right.

CASE STUDIES

MEN OF QUALITY
DON'T FEAR
EQUALITY

BELIEVE
WOMEN

DEOFHISTORY.ORG

BEONTHERIGHTSIDEOFHISTORY.ORG

GIRLS JUST WANT TO HAVE
FUNDAMENTAL RIGHTS

WE'RE ONLY

Could you please elaborate on your research/development process? How important is it in the overall scheme of things and how do your findings influence the final design work?

Historical context and contemporary politics were important in understanding this project. 'Be on the Right Side of History' was created when Donald Trump won the United States presidency. Women all over the world were rightfully angry and disappointed in the electoral outcome and took to the streets in protest. The protest that transpired in 2017 was one of the biggest civil rights movements in western history. This project was created to honour this movement and the women, both past and present, who have fought for change.

How do you typically work and communicate with your client or overcome differences in opinion to achieve the best results? Following which, what do you hope to inspire/change in audiences from this project?

This project was created to inspire change and evoke emotion. I hope that women see the work and feel empowered to use their voices and take on the patriarchy bravely, just like the women featured in this project have. As women, we are often, understandably, afraid of the retribution we face when we use our voices. It can be scary, but the voices of many are more powerful than the voices of a few.

How do the skills/abilities of a designer come into play, particularly in projects for the greater good? What have you personally learned/taken away from this project?

Design skills and abilities are crucial if you want to create meaningful design. Companies all over the world have learned this. It's why Apple and Google spend so much money on their branding. But as designers, we should not limit our skills to just selling things for businesses. If good design is so powerful and effective, why not use it to also inspire change?

There have been rising discussions on designers' roles and responsibilities over the years. What do you think is/are the core values/mentality designers today need to be equipped with in order to foster a better world?

It's naive to think that every project you do will be ethical or align with your moral values. That's (sadly) not the world we live in. As an art director, I've been in tough positions before where I've tried to convince clients to take a moral position to no avail. I've taken it so far that I've been fired off projects. It's a double-edged sword working from an ethical position, and at the end of the day, we do need to support ourselves and our families. As such, it needs to be a personal choice, how far you're willing to bend. I do think, however, that designers should know what issues are important to them and be educated on them. That way, if you do face an issue with a client, you can respectfully inform them where you're coming form and explain how that perspective can actually help advance them in the world today.

Ⓓ

Autism Awareness Posters

CLIENT
Nelson Occupational Therapy Centre

Over the period of the Movement Control Order (MCO) or lockdown in Malaysia due to the pandemic, the team at IDEOLOGY DESIGN STUDIO decided to kickstart a social project where the team designed (absolutely free) posters for 30 selected small businesses who were struggling by not being able to operate, in hopes of helping them through the power of design. Its autism awareness poster series was part of the efforts, created for the Nelson Occupational Therapy Centre. Each poster set out to educate the public on what autism is, which is why the visuals were designed using an easily digestible approach to help people learn about the symptoms of autism.

"Designers today should know that there are always more solutions than problems in this world. As such, we don't need to stick to one design style or just one solution."

Could you please elaborate on your research/development process? How important is it in the overall scheme of things and how do your findings influence the final design work?

Our creative process does not only apply to primary research online, but it also involves what we see and what we learn from other people's stories and how we communicate with different people in our daily lives. You'll never know who is going to inspire you on your upcoming projects. We think human interactions play a huge part in inspiring our projects.

How do you typically work and communicate with your client or overcome differences in opinion to achieve the best results? Following which, what do you hope to inspire/change in audiences from this project?

Our communication with clients always starts from listening — listening to problems and obstacles that they are facing, or trying to find out the problems that their market is facing. The client's opinion is important in a project, but to us, what is most important is what works best for their market. We always try our best to educate our clients that we are the bridge between the brand and their target market, and their personal preferences come second.

How do the skills/abilities of a designer come into play, particularly in projects for the greater good? What have you personally learned/taken away from this project?

Designers today should know that there are always more solutions than problems in this world. As such, we don't need to stick to just one design style or just one solution.

Dr Giraffe
Book Series

Explaining an illness to a child, whether it is common or serious, is no easy feat. While it is something every parent must do, knowing what to say and how to say it can be a huge challenge, as they often simply do not have the medical knowledge needed to provide much-needed comfort — and this is where Dr Giraffe comes in. Using simple words and pictures, and grounded in medical truth, each book in the series by Studio Rejane Dal Bello tells a story about one childhood disease, ranging from common ailments to rare conditions. To mum and dad's relief, Dr Giraffe can do what they perhaps cannot: help young patients make sense of what they are going through, in a way that is clear, medically accurate and (no less importantly) pleasant to read.

alf-half

A little story about cleft palate and lip

land OF THE big

A little story about leukaemia

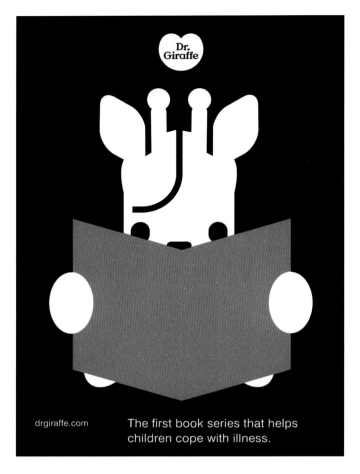

drgiraffe.com

The first book series that helps children cope with illness.

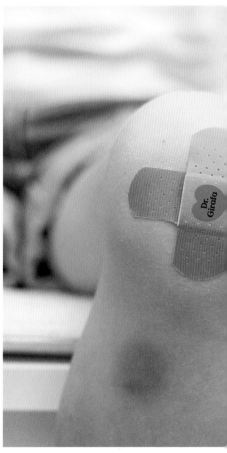

Could you please elaborate on your research/development process? How important is it in the overall scheme of things and how do your findings influence the final design work?

A good brief from the client goes a long way. After that, I spend time researching the real meaning behind the clients' words and intentions. This is then translated into a design project and its consequences. Understanding the realm of the project first will define the boundaries of what to design. Creativity is limitless, so defining the core and its purpose is essential for focusing on the right path.

How do you typically work and communicate with your client or overcome differences in opinion to achieve the best results? Following which, what do you hope to inspire/change in audiences from this project?

We make sure that we play back what our clients have asked of us, laying out our thinking and developing it further with their input. To me, thinking along and pushing with them, not against them, is key. From their perspective, we build our conclusions — supported by conversations.

How do the skills/abilities of a designer come into play, particularly in projects for the greater good? What have you personally learned/taken away from this project?

Typically, projects for the greater good result in hardly any monetary compensation (in my experience), so what is left is your love for the cause and how much or honestly you can add to it. Being close to what you like and the issues you care about are essential, especially if you are not going to be paid for your time or effort. This only happens when you truly enjoy what you do.

For our balloon repairs,
We must pay with our hair!
So every head is as bare as can be.

It might seem quite funny
That we don't pay in money
But that's how we do it, you see!

Alzheimer Nederland

CLIENT
Alzheimer Nederland

Alzheimer's and other forms of dementia are presenting the human race with one of its toughest challenges, driving organisations like Alzheimer Nederland to work hard in raising awareness and funds for vital research. However, times have been hard and competition for donors has never been tougher. Having met patients, families and carers who have experienced the disease first-hand, the team at Studio Dumbar developed a strong and instantly recognisable identity with 'vanishing points' to visualise the effects of dementia, inspiring some viewers to see them as a source of light and hope. The most important moment in the process came when the identity was shared with patients and carers, whose feedback was overwhelmingly positive.

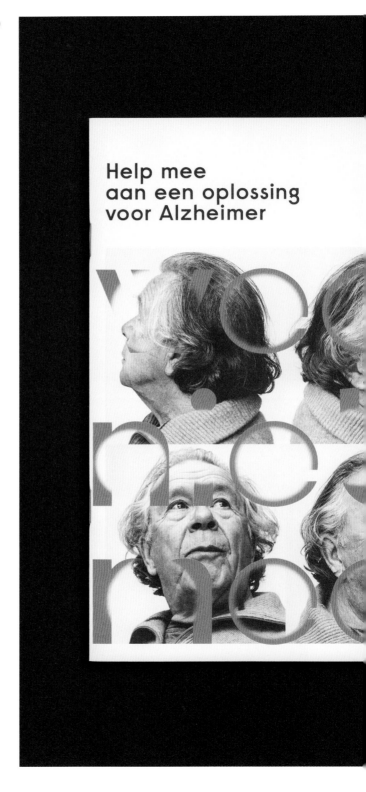

Could you please elaborate on your research/development process? How important is it in the overall scheme of things and how do your findings influence the final design work?

The research/development process starts with trying to understand the organisation we are working for. And with understanding, we mean beyond grasping the brief, like its deeper motives and interests. Once we understand all that, we try to boil it down to the pure essence, distilling all the complexities and dynamics of the organisation into just a few words, making it simple to understand and relate to. After that, we go into the 'define' phase. This is the phase we breathe in and brings us to a clear starting point for the creative process. It gives us a sense of direction and provides a basis for the most asked questions in all the reviews that follow: 'why?'

How do you typically work and communicate with your client or overcome differences in opinion to achieve the best results? Following which, what do you hope to inspire/change in audiences from this project?

Differences of opinion are an opportunity or a necessity to get to know each other better. If it occurs, you need to try to understand what is behind the difference of opinion; where does it come from? If you're not on the same page, perhaps something has been overlooked or not understood well enough. It is very important in such a case, to

"Don't wait for others. Do the right thing yourself."

be open about it and see how you can get in sync again. If you succeed in that, it will bring you closer to the right answer. The most important thing is not to have an ego that gets in the way. You have to have an open mind in looking at differences.

How do the skills/abilities of a designer come into play, particularly in projects for the greater good? What have you personally learned/taken away from this project?

As far as required skills are concerned, there is no difference between projects for the greater good or a commercial assignment. It might be that a designer is more engaged and driven, but the skills required are the same. You need to have the creative power and imagination to express the essence of a subject or organisation, to bring it to life. And in our case, you also need to be able to work together, to be open to being part of a team, reviewing work together, trying to find the best possible solution, looking beyond your individual interests and talent.

Is het dementie?

alzheimer nederland

meer
weten
over

Als thuis wonen niet meer gaat

alzheimer nederland

niet
meer
thuis

Sneller
naar betere
oplossingen

alzheimer nederland

Relief Watch — Humanitarian Accountability, Reimagined

CLIENT
Overseas Development Institute,
Humanity United

In creating a new independent service for recipients of humanitarian assistance, the concept for the Relief Watch — Humanitarian Accountability, Reimagined project was developed through a collaborative and inclusive design process. At its core, Relief Watch allows aid recipients to provide qualitative feedback on the assistance and services they receive, and collates their responses to provide useful and actionable feedback to humanitarian staff and donors. In doing so, it works to facilitate a more direct relationship between humanitarian organisations and the communities with which they work. On completion of the project, Relief Watch evolved into an independent charity called Loop, whose mission is shifting the power dynamics within the humanitarian and development sectors.

Could you please elaborate on your research/development process? How important is it in the overall scheme of things and how do your findings influence the final design work?

The design process is not a one-size fits all one — it's a set of methods and tools that we can choose from and arrange in an order that is appropriate for the challenge at hand. In this project, the team adapted the traditional design process to ensure that the perspectives of aid recipients during research and prototyping were sought and incorporated into the concept development, ethically and with their informed consent. This meant creating spaces that people in refugee and IDP camps in Iraq could safely and voluntarily visit, and engage with prototypes without fear of reprisal. The team inverted the design process to ensure that the fidelity of prototypes of compliant or feedback mechanisms were such that they provided a real channel for people's suggestions and opinions to be directed to the organisations responsible for providing services in their areas.

How do you typically work and communicate with your client or overcome differences in opinion to achieve the best results? Following which, what do you hope to inspire/change in audiences from this project?

Differences in opinion should be celebrated, and encouraged. They offer an opportunity to test and find the ideal solution. As designers, we are trained to manage ambiguity and experientially test ideas without bias. When moments of difference arise with clients, we try to break ideas up into their smallest components. Then, together with the client, we find avenues to test these components in isolation, and later, in combination with each other. This gives the idea the best opportunity to be informed from both an expert's point of view, as well as the target user behaviour. Together with clients, we triage the findings to evaluate how best to continue.

How do the skills/abilities of a designer come into play, particularly in projects for the greater good? What have you personally learned/taken away from this project?

The design process and empathy-building exercises are no substitute for having designers on the team who are as-close-as-possible to the target user group. Design teams should ideally be open, diverse, and consist of people who have experienced the problem first-hand. In this project, this meant ensuring that the design team included people from crises-affected countries, and refugee backgrounds as often and as early as possible.

Jólan van der Wiel
& Nick Verstand

Ⓗ

Smart Distancing System

As a creative means of visualising social distancing in public spaces, Dutch artists Jólan van der Wiel and Nick Verstand developed the Smart Distancing System, through which a combination of motion-tracking technology and computer-controlled lasers draw playful lines on the ground, varying according to the presence of passers-by. The system sets out to make it easier for individuals to move safely and intelligently through public spaces, as we navigate gatherings in the new normal. Through circles, shapes, arrows and/or lines, the minimum safe distance between people is distinctly illustrated, making it safer and also more fun for people to visit crowded places like train stations, airports, shops, fairs, restaurants, and even festivals or clubs in the future.

Could you please elaborate on your research/development process? How important is it in the overall scheme of things and how do your findings influence the final design work?

We like to react on what happens around us with new ideas that can improve lives. Technology often plays a role in this.

How do you typically work and communicate with your client or overcome differences in opinion to achieve the best results? Following which, what do you hope to inspire/change in audiences from this project?

We mostly start with drawings or animations to convince clients and audiences before investing in the development process.

How do the skills/abilities of a designer come into play, particularly in projects for the greater good? What have you personally learned/taken away from this project?

It's all about following the gut feeling and doing it fast!

Kosuke Takahashi

NIN_NIN

CLIENT
Ory Laboratory Inc.

NIN_NIN is a 'body sharing' robot that sets out to share body functions using technology. Through the robot, people can share their 'sight' with the visually impaired using cameras, which would enable the former to help the latter if they are unable to leave their homes; or share a foreign language with foreigners using a microphone. Developed in collaboration with Ory Laboratory Inc., product designer Kosuke Takahashi sets out to ensure the safety of the visually impaired, promote the employment of vulnerable groups, solve problems relating to loneliness, and promote kindness for the greater good. At present, NIN_NIN is being used by several local governments to support the community, including those with disabilities, in terms of tourism or shopping.

Could you please elaborate on your research/development process? How important is it in the overall scheme of things and how do your findings influence the final design work?

It is surprising that even in this day and age, the visually impaired still have to cross junctions/intersections using their intuition and courage. Upon further investigation, we found that they face challenges in various other situations, such as not being able to select a drink from a vending machine or stop a cab. This was why NIN_NIN was born. By connecting to the robot through a smartphone app, you can share your sight with the visually impaired. During the development stage, we considered various robot shapes, but decided to go with a shoulder-mounted robot in response to feedback from the visually impaired that it would be better if the robot was not attached to the face, or did not get in the way of the hand holding a cane. As a result, it has become an 'attachment 'for various people. This is beneficial not only for the visually impaired, but also for many other people. As the culture of 'Body Sharing' spreads, you can share the functions of your body and have experiences that were not possible before, the spirit of helping each other by doing what we can will spread.

How do you typically work and communicate with your Client or overcome differences in opinion to achieve the best results? Following which, what do you hope to inspire/change in audiences from this project?

In the early stages of the project, not many understood the value of the system, but as more and more new ways of using it were created through prototyping, everyone began to realise its true value. Through the robot, we hope to increase the number of new experiences created by sharing body functions in various places.

How do the skills/abilities of a designer come into play, particularly in projects for the greater good? What have you personally learned/taken away from this project?

Prototyping allowed us to see the scalability of our ideas. By prototyping with ambiguous use case scenarios and lending them out to various users, we found many ways to use the robot beyond our imagination.

PLASTIC PAPER

It is no secret that single-use plastic bags are choking our cities and planet. Designer Sho Shibuya of PLACEHOLDER was inspired to act for the preservation of everyday design and raise a call to give greater care to the objects we use by reusing them and wasting less. He also sought to find happiness and inspiration in the little acts of art and creativity we would otherwise miss. Plastic Paper was a passion project that merged cultural observation with ecological activism. At its core, it is a yearbook that preserves anonymous design heritage while nudging single-use plastics into retirement. Since the project began, it has evolved into a broad-range creative platform for sustainability projects, and the Plastic Paper brand has been used to explore new materials, process designs, and other ways to reduce plastic waste.

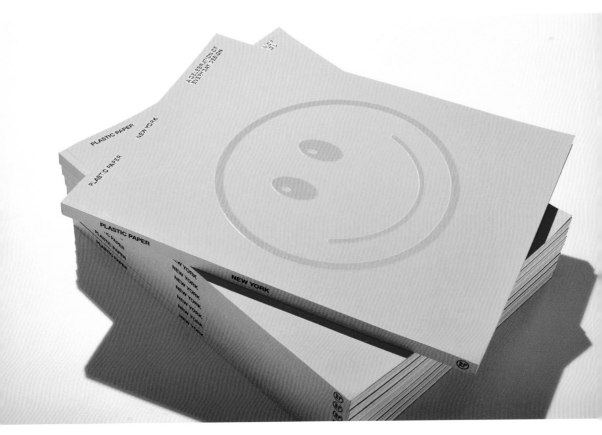

Could you please elaborate on your research/development process? How important is it in the overall scheme of things and how do your findings influence the final design work?

The research phase is an integral part of the process. Once we are confident of moving forward with production, the process is simple and informational. We prefer telling messages over visuals and typography. We use this platform to express our creative power and bring a positive impact to our world.

How do you typically work and communicate with your client or overcome differences in opinion to achieve the best results? Following which, what do you hope to inspire/change in audiences from this project?

We hope to share what we learned from the Plastic Paper project with others. For instance, we had to convince one of the start-up clients we were working with to use glass, aluminum or a refillable programme instead of disposable plastic packaging. It is never easy, and a lot of conflicts arise. Although we run the risk of losing the client, we do not want our actions to be contradictory. We hope that businesses will be able to coexist with environmentally-friendly manufacturing and processes.

How do the skills/abilities of a designer come into play, particularly in projects for the greater good? What have you personally learned/taken away from this project?

I learned that people are always willing to lend a hand if you are humble or using your creative power for good. Creating everything based on continuous research is the key to sharing your story widely and making an impact. I used to think creating a cool visual is the most important, but now, it is secondary. The fundamental things are concept and message.

There have been rising discussions on designers' roles and responsibilities over the years. What do you think is/are the core values/mentality designers today need to be equipped with in order to foster a better world?

In the past, I used to believe that graphic designers could be viewed as artists. Now, as technology continues to get better and faster, it is easier to create cool visuals. You need to think about the cause you want to highlight through your project. It helps if you think about the broader conclusion. Design is about problem-solving, and as graphic designers, we continue to face tough fundamental challenges. Reducing environmental impact is one of them.

There are objects that are both anonymous and instantly recognizable. They're the mundane pieces of urban flotsam that alone mean nothing, but together contribute to the essential milieu of a place. You may or may not know the specific origin of these things — the Anthora coffee cup, the MetroCard, "Post No Bills" stenciled on green plywood — but you absolutely recognize them. These designs don't belong to anyone; not even the ones with a definite design lineage. They belong to and give form to the image of the city as a whole. They have graduated from the specific to the general vernacular.

This book is about one of those objects — the single-use plastic bag — that has become a canvas for a range of anonymous expressions of design. You see them hanging from the handlebars of every delivery person's electrified bike. They're snarled in the leafless trees. They're wrapped around cyclists' leather saddles. The smiley face bag, the quintuple Thank You, the purple flowers; these are as much a piece of the visual landscape of the city as Milton Glaser's I♥NY or Massimo Vignelli's subway map. And while this book is focused on New York City, cities from Tokyo to Terre Haute have their own language of mundane iconography, and we encourage you to pay attention to them, to investigate their history and discover the story they tell.

Let this book remind you that despite their role in defining the visual design of our city, the era of the single-use plastic bag is well overdue. We're eager to see this prolific veteran of our daily design experience retire, and make room for a new surface for expression.

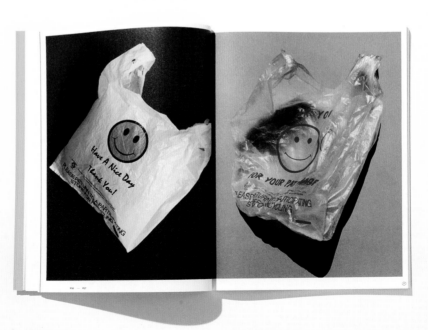

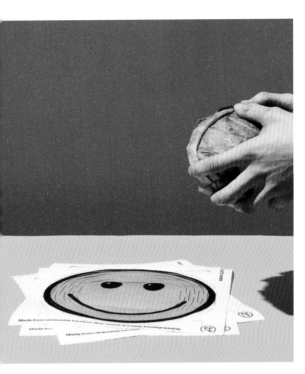
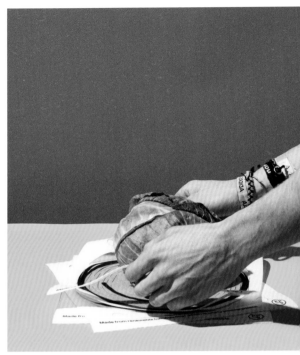

Notpla

CLIENT
Notpla

8 million tonnes of plastic are dumped into the oceans every year, which is where Notpla comes in — a revolutionary, seaweed-based material that naturally decomposes in around 6 weeks. Superunion created the new name and brand to reflect the company's vision for the future and promote Notpla as a leading household name at the forefront of environmental sustainability. The new identity focuses on the brand's core mission: to make packaging disappear. The animated logo reflects a vessel that can be filled with liquid and when it is emptied, the exterior disappears, just like its packaging. Notpla is built on the idea that its products will change the world and the team communicated its bold and brave intention in a clear and compelling way.

Could you please elaborate on your research/development process? How important is it in the overall scheme of things and how do your findings influence the final design work?

It is important to have an understanding of the immediate competitor landscape, but inter-sector research is also key. That said, we find the best insights usually come from in-depth conversations with our client. Our research drew us to the unusual practice of defining the brand by what it isn't — not plastic. What makes Notpla different is exactly what it isn't, and that's the beauty of it. Also, the global environmental issue of single-use plastic is so huge and pressing, it made sense to directly state this in the brand name.

How do you typically work and communicate with your client or overcome differences in opinion to achieve the best results? Following which, what do you hope to inspire/change in audiences from this project?

At Superunion, we believe in the power of ideas to create positive and meaningful change in the world, and Notpla could not be a better representation of this. We hope to change behaviours in our audiences and Notpla is tackling the huge challenge of single-use plastics. The ultimate aim is to stop billions of single-use plastic packaging from ever

being made by providing a positive alternative. We believe Notpla has the potential of turning the tide on plastic waste.

How do the skills/abilities of a designer come into play, particularly in projects for the greater good? What have you personally learned/taken away from this project?

Brands have a defining role in the world and in how they impact society. As designers, we are problem solvers. We have a desire to fix something and this means helping brands to define what makes them unique and to deliver greater value to the world around them.

There have been rising discussions on designers' roles and responsibilities over the years. What do you think is/are the core values/mentality designers today need to be equipped with in order to foster a better world?

The best companies are those that benefit people and society the most. Brands are being judged by their value to society, and as designers working with these brands, we have to be aware of our own actions. The ideas and brands that we create have impact, and we must ensure that the impact we make is a positive one.

Series A — Forget Fashion

Working with non-profit football club Champions Without Borders e.V., graphic designer Timm Hartmann developed the idea of designing football shirts in collaboration with refugee children and young adults. Two workshops took place, in which 24 refugee children aged between 9 and 16 years old, learned about the structure of professional football jerseys and the graphic elements that create the jerseys' distinctive style, giving them an insight into the creative process of a designer. At the same time, they got to evaluate their own strengths and see their backgrounds as an opportunity. The resulting collection, Series A, was presented as an art exhibition to raise awareness about refugees.

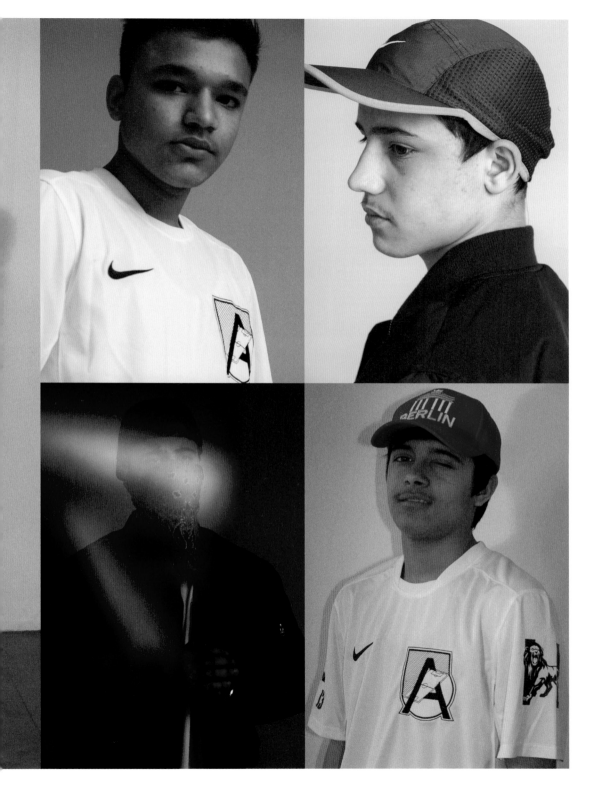

Could you please elaborate on your research/development process? How important is it in the overall scheme of things and how do your findings influence the final design work?

Our first step in every project is a thorough research phase, especially when it comes to more complex problems. With this phase, we are able to communicate with our clients at eye level and, as designers, provide a different perspective on things. This helps us immensely in getting a feel for the scope of a task and to expose any possible weaknesses in the concept. At the same time, it provides us with the basic framework for our design,

which, by following fixed principles, doesn't become arbitrary.

For Public Positions, it was important for us to really comprehend the project's circumstances and to have a deeper understanding of the needs and complex situations of the participants or collaborators. This created a basis for discussion and open exchange which, at least for me, has always brought new, surprising twists and turns to the design. Through workshops with children, you can always come up with truly amazing design solutions.

حمزة برهان
HAMTA H. BOURHAN
13

Series B —
Poster Stories

For graphic designer Timm Hart-mann's Series B project, 10 young refugees created a series of post-ers based on their current hob-bies, memories and hopes for the future. The posters were designed in collaboration with Berlin-based graphic designer Florian Sei-del and accompanied by video portraits shot by Berlin-based photographer Nora Heinisch. For this project, posters were chosen as the main medium due to their lightness and mobility, enabling the refugees to take their final work with them wherever they went next. The idea of the project was based on the simple fact that something as simple as a beloved poster has the potential to transform every new space into one that feels like home.

How do you typically work and communicate with your clients or overcome differences in opinion to achieve the best results? Following which, what do you hope to inspire/change in audiences from this project?

Series B was less about impressing or influencing customers or arty people, but about creating a workshop and a product with and for the refugee children who took part in this project. I have my own publishing house (www. presentbooks.de) and, in addition to various jobs as a graphic designer, I mainly produce a street magazine called Karuna Kompass, which is sold by homeless people in Berlin and actively supports them. You could say that 99% of the time, I never have to deal with customers directly. So, it is really rare that there are different opinions that cannot be discussed, but as a tip for tackling this 'problem', I can only give the following advice: only show your clients work that you are 100% behind. Never show something half-cut or too abstract, and it always helps to get ideas beforehand or to find out in conversation what your client finds visually attractive.
(Florian Seidel)

How do the skills/abilities of a designer come into play, particularly in projects for the greater good? What have you personally learned/taken away from this project?

As a designer, you have the abilities to present a problem, theme or issue to a broader audience by using the tools of visual communication. These tools enable designers to take responsibility by contributing to issues that are socially or politically relevant, by creating lower thresholds, providing accessibility, pushing boundaries, etc. We have learned from this project that it is always important to us to take care of topics that surround us as human beings in our personal life and activate others to deal with these respective topics too. Ultimately, the role of a designer is not fixed. It is more about your personal choice for what, for whom, and how you want to use your abilities.
(Büro Bum Bum)

Series C — Positivisions

In a time of increasing complexity and radicalisation of our societies, Berlin design collective Büro Bum Bum — then consisting of Sebastian Bareis, Eric Dannebaum, Dirk Gössler, Jan Kapitän, Matthias Klinger and Pascal Schönegg — together with graphic designer Timm Hartmann, organised an exhibition revolving around alternative visions, collective ways of thinking and the power of the positive. Besides discussing questions like "how do my private and public positions differ?" and "how can positive visions be reconceived and promoted?" in joint workshops, many notable creatives and influential people like Joseph Beuys, with his Guide to the Good Life, and Dutch artist Jeanne van Heeswijk also participated in their search for answers.

There have been rising discussions on designers' roles and responsibilities over the years. What do you think is/are the core values/mentality designers today need to be equipped with in order to foster a better world?

To me, design is an expression of a world in which we want to live. Starting as a designer, I was particularly interested in the political and social interconnections within visual communication. Precisely because it is traditionally part of visual communication to question the established, to debate on how we live, I became interested in developing concepts for new forms of living in the cultural and social environment – finding a way to connect these to more commercialised ways of thinking. For me, design does not simply mean the process of conception and planning of material objects, but also the process of designing immaterial modes of action, such as political strategies and social practices. One way to create new forms of living is to reflect on the future in the sense of anticipating what may come and to find ways with which we can positively contribute to this new design.

EARTH CARE

PEOPLE CARE
RESOURCE
SHARE

Gro(w)up
Diver—city
Tr(us)t
Coll—active
T(own)
L—earn
Res(our)ces
T—each
T(all)k
Recl(aim)
Prod—user

Public Positions
Series C: Postfictions

Büro Bum Bum
Edition of 100

Item: Poster 002
Title: Earth care

www.publicpositions.com

Public Positions
Series C: Postfictions

Büro Bum Bum
Edition of 100

Item: Poster 001
Title: Wor(l)d

www.publicpositions.com

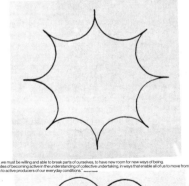

"...In order to begin, we must be willing and able to break parts of ourselves, to have new room for new ways of being. It goes back to the idea of becoming active in the understanding of collective undertaking, in ways that enable all of us to move from being passive consumers to active producers of our everyday conditions."

Public Positions
Series C: Postfictions

Büro Bum Bum
Edition of 100

Item: Poster 003
Title: Active consumer

www.publicpositions.com

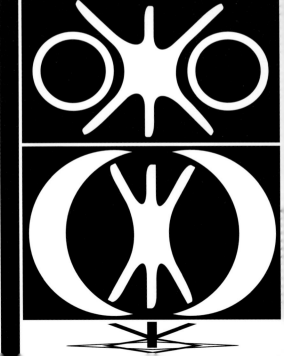

Monarch Brand Identity

CLIENT
Monarch by SimplePractice

Paladar was brought in to build the Monarch brand identity from the ground up and then extend a robust visual language across the brand's core touch points. The team designed a logo inspired by the flight path of a monarch butterfly, complemented by a colour palette and type system that felt welcoming and flexible. A system for expressive typography was used as emphasis in storytelling, with the pattern language adding depth and warmth throughout the brand and its touchpoints. Rebecca Clarke's illustrations formed the heart of the work, translating the studio's vision into a surreal and inclusive portrayal of everyday people and mental health.

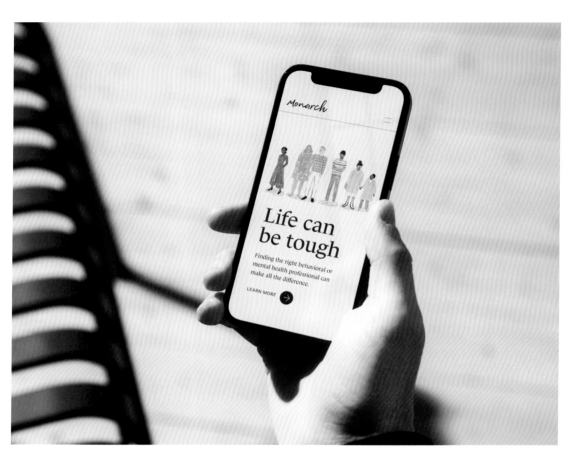

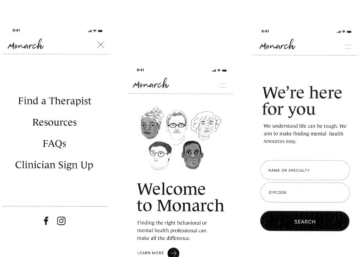

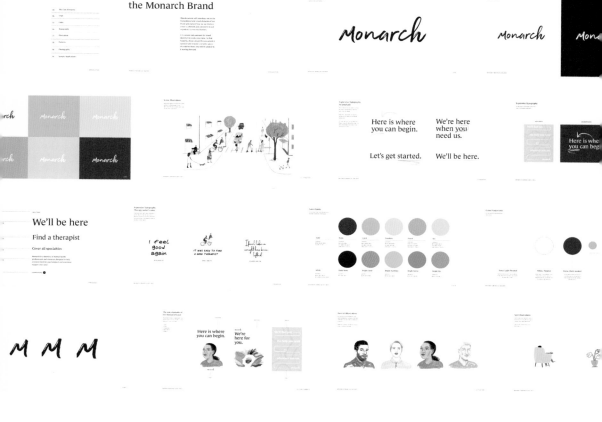

Could you please elaborate on your research/development process? How important is it in the overall scheme of things and how do your findings influence the final design work?

All of our design work is first rooted in strategy: the who, the what, the how, and most importantly, the why. Research plays a role in this immersion stage for us and we conduct brand workshops, 1:1 stakeholder interviews, customer interviews, and broad research into the space and product. Our process is deeply influenced by the strategy we develop in collaboration with our clients; it's our shared language and North Star for what we create together.

How do you typically work and communicate with your client or overcome differences in opinion to achieve the best results? Following which, what do you hope to inspire/change in audiences from this project?

Trust and communication are key. We do a lot of upfront work to establish trust with our clients: we give them insight into our process so they understand our thinking and we're honest about our beliefs and capabilities. Tactically, we spend a lot of time with them answering questions and finding alignment while also investing hours of early collaborative workshops that set us up for success. We always bias towards face-to-face communication to overcome any differences and try to keep an open dialogue about the work. Branding can be a lot like therapy! We always try to convey that we're on this journey together and we're all ultimately invested in the same thing: beautiful work that has an impact for our clients (and the world around us).

How do the skills/abilities of a designer come into play, particularly in projects for the greater good? What have you personally learned/taken away from this project?

Design has the capacity to make people really feel something. We have an enormous potential (and responsibility) as designers to solve problems with empathy and encourage people to care for the world around them. With Monarch, a core goal of ours was to destigmatise mental health and support people on their path to wellness. First and foremost, we wanted anyone who came to Monarch to feel safe. We worked hard to put ourselves in the shoes of those who might feel alienated or people who were looking for a therapist in a state of crisis. We aimed to create a design system that felt safe and like a breath of fresh air. For us, this meant warm colours, hand-drawn elements, and diverse portraits of everyday people at all stages in their lives.

There have been rising discussions on designers' roles and responsibilities over the years. What do you think is/are the core values/mentality designers today need to be equipped with in order to foster a better world?

Leading with empathy: Designers can facilitate understanding and tangibility by embedding our design work with qualities that people can feel on the other end.

A collaborative and humble mindset: We see value in coming at problems from a place of curiosity and open-mindedness. Silos create tunnel vision; we are excited about the strength of multidisciplinary teams working together.

Operating from a place of reciprocity and abundance: We deeply believe that our core unit is 'we' rather than 'I', as all flourishing is mutual. As a community, we should be supporting and encouraging other creatives and lifting each other up.

We're here for you.

Monarch

STORIES

① One Bite Design Studio
② crafting plastics! studio
③ WeTransfer

One Bite
Design Studio

Changing the Faces of Spaces,
One Creative Bite at a Time

When it comes to making a difference, many tend to bite off more than they can chew. Although one can set off with the very best of intentions driven by the fact that the smallest of actions can cascade into bigger outcomes, it takes both acumen and ability to materialise ambitious projects that resonate with audiences on a deep and visceral level.

One Bite Design Studio is one such entity that has been creating a meaningful impact through design for good. By bringing together a community of architects, designers, community outreach managers and event managers across its offices in Hong Kong (China) and Singapore (Singapore), the architecture-based multidisciplinary company strives to bridge the gaps between space, place and society by constantly exploring the synergies between its stakeholders.

Managing director Alan Cheung, whose design career has spanned 14 years in Hong Kong (China), London (UK) and New York (USA), co-founded One Bite Design Studio with partner and fellow architect Sarah Mui back in 2015 when they could no longer ignore the niggling feeling that something had to give — and that it was time to do things little bit differently.

"Architects are trained to use creativity to find solutions to a problem. In today's world where social and urban issues are so complex that they cannot be solved by one discipline alone, I felt that we should not just use our architectural training to simply build another piece of architecture. It seems more effective to apply our ability of facilitation to solve more deep-rooted problems in a collaborative manner. Achieving spatial equality and tackling ageing are my core visions that continue to motivate us along the way."

In the aftermath of the 2020 pandemic, One Bite Design Studio's philosophy has become more poignant and relevant than ever. With health, safety and well-being becoming key concerns for communities all over the world, the face of architecture has slowly but surely been changing. Many of the details that people used to take for granted are now being considered more carefully, such as the boundaries between private and public or indoor and outdoor spaces, to minimise contact and contamination if necessary without hindering flow or freedom of movement. Beyond brick and mortar, the emphasis has been moving towards purposeful designs that serve to improve life in more holistic ways.

For Cheung, he defines designing for good as a daily practice. "It can be very intangible, where design empowers spatial equality. On the other hand, it can be as tangible as creating an inclusive park for all ages and abilities. Designing for good reflects the social and environmental re-sponsibility that any designer/architect should carry and practise. We are surrounded by design every day and every minute, so there should be no excuse for us not to use it as a tool to create a better world."

AN OBJECT × MOBILE WARDROBE SERIES (i)

Underlined by the concept of anonymity, 'An Object' was a pack-and-go social bicycle project that was initiated by One Bite Design Studio to subtly 'intervene' in various public spaces across Hong Kong, China. By placing benches and tables within the designated spaces according to the site-specific landscape, passers-by were provided with the opportunity to stop for a chit-chat and connect, even if briefly. 'An Object' was also featured as part of a collaboration with Look Matters for its Mobile Wardrobe series, in advocating for the reduction of fast fashion consumption. It was transformed into a second-hand clothes container for a series of exchange events.

JUNK! WOODWORKING (ii–iii)

In 2018, tens of thousands of trees, including many old and valuable ones, were toppled by Typhoon Mangkhut in Hong Kong, China. To utilise and recycle the fallen wood, the Hong Kong Art Promotion Office collaborated with One Bite Design Studio and the Hong Kong Sculpture Society to launch the 'Junk! Woodworking' campaign, which included a woodworking exhibition at the 2019 Hong Kong Flower Show, an 'Adopt A Log' brainstorming session, as well as an educational programme for primary and secondary school students to raise public awareness and appreciation for the trees by inviting them to explore woodworking further.

(i)

One Bite Design Studio's projects are as inspiring as they are intriguing. Besides curating and organising a diverse range of events around cities to find and reconnect the missing links between architecture and the people who live within them, the company actively advocates the latter's rights to high-quality urban spaces by planning programmes that allow them to re-imagine the environment around them. In addition to its architecture and interiors projects, it also conducts research and public engagement programmes on issues such as mental health to educate city dwellers from all walks of life. Its visual language seamlessly blends form with function to pique curiosity, encourage exploration and deliver happiness.

Cheung acknowledges that it can often be challenging to achieve a balance between commercial objectives and altruistic ones. "I used to have the perception that they clashed, to be honest. However, the world has changed. Today, we know that a purpose-driven business can create an impact while simultaneously maintaining the necessary viability for the company to grow. The sustainable growth of an economy relies heavily on the wellness of its people and the balance between societal and environmental development. As such, our work tries to advocate for the need of balance and win-win conditions."

From pop-ups that tackle the phenomenon of vacant ground-level shops to meet the growing demands for community spaces in a city known for its astronomical rent to wood-working workshops that invite the public to see old trees in a new light and appreciate their true value, One Bite Design Studio's range of ideas have been extensive and compelling. Through its projects, it hopes to demonstrate that agility in design solutions can create insightful solutions to the social and environmental problems today.

(ii)

At the company's core, Cheung does not believe in singular effort, taking a collaborative and participatory approach to bridge multiple disciplines in every project. "Collaborative culture is in our DNA. Internally, we have a diversified team composition. Different expertise gives us the opportunity to work with other backgrounds, injecting vibrancy into our ideas and teamwork. Externally, it is essential to collaborate with stakeholders and other experts so that we can all arrive at all-rounded solutions."

Recalling the company's projects so far with fondness, Cheung finds it hard to choose the one that he likes best. "We always have a number of exciting projects going on, but if I had to pick a favourite, it would be the Siu Hei Court Sports Ground, a revamped rooftop public space completed in 2020. The project was the fourth one we worked on with the same client, involving the revitalisation of under-utilised rooftop public spaces in degenerated housing estates. Local students were involved in the process and we experimented with an unstructured play-space design, which has since generated some positive and creative feedback."

In this ever-evolving city, where traditional Asian values remain tightly intertwined with modern concepts and Western culture, cultivating new thought patterns and habits within certain sections of society can be a complex task. The introduction of the unfamiliar will always be met with some level of resistance, but it takes courage and patience to persevere until the end — qualities that One Bite Design Studio has in spades.

"With everything that is going on today, our built environment is in need of more joyful spaces than ever to counteract the growing tension around us."

DESIGN DISTRICT HONG KONG (i–ii)

One Bite Design Studio curated a series of placemaking installations and social campaigns to transform Wan Chai, one of 18 districts in Hong Kong (China) steeped in rich cultural history, into a joyful neighbourhood with an open-air gallery celebrating creativity and design. Working together with Design District Hong Kong (#ddHK) as its creative partner, as well as over 20 other design and community groups, the collaborative experimental journey set out to develop possibilities for even more creative placemaking collaborations in the future.

SIU HEI COURT SPORTSGROUND (iii)

The Siu Hei Court Sportsground revitalisation project set out to inject energy and joy into a decrepit rooftop space, transforming an ordinary and dated sportsground into an intergenerational play space. Inspired by the name of the estate, which rhymes with the Chinese words for 'smile' and 'laughter', One Bite Design Studio's design work aimed to evoke a sense of happiness and positivity. Besides creating a new identity for Siu Hei, the project also demonstrated how untapped potential in rooftop sportgrounds can be unlocked to provide more meaningful and fulfilling experiences for all.

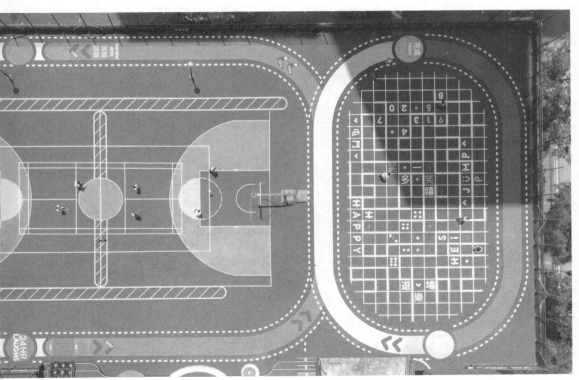

PROJECT HOUSE (i–ii)

One Bite Design Studio's Project House is driven by a pop-up strategy to tackle the phenomenon of vacant ground-level shops and the growing demand for community spaces. Each pop-up is an opportunity for NGOs, social enterprises, local start-ups, independent groups and building owners to experiment with new ideas and revive the community through knowledge sharing.

COMMUNITY EVENT AT KENNEDY TOWN (iii–iv)

As part of its ongoing efforts to bring people in neighbourhoods together, One Bite Design Studio worked with Caritas Mok Cheung Shui Kun Community Centre and iDiscover to creatively transform a brewery into a community hub, brought to life through an art exhibition, local crafts workshop, a storytelling session and a pop-up chillax space for the local dwellers in Kennedy Town.

"When it comes to designing for good, we cannot expect to make a total impression or change people in seconds. Creating a change in perceptions or behaviours always takes longer than expected, which can be really challenging. Interestingly enough, this is probably the very reason we call ourselves 'One Bite'. We always have to remind ourselves to take one bite at a time until people are empowered enough to change."

So far, Cheung is proud and hopeful that the public has responded well to the work. "As far as we know, people usually perceive our projects as colourful and progressive, in that we usually suggest new approaches. Some of them have even commented that we always manage to surprise them in some way. All this feedback is very crucial for our team to learn and persist. With everything that is going on today, our built environment is in need of more joyful spaces than ever to counteract the growing tension around us."

As an architect who has managed to expand his design discipline in a variety of enriching ways over the years, Cheung is forever changed. "Designing for good has sharpened my skillsets to observe and empathise with the community in a significant way. I no longer only focus on the aesthetics of design, but have become more aware of and sensitive to what people need, as well as the strategic relationships between humanity and nature. I also now believe in 'living for a cause but not for applause'. As a designer, we were trained to glow in the era of star architects. However, it only gave us the excuse to avoid shouldering our social and environmental responsibilities as a design professional. If we had only learned to step back and become facilitators sooner, we could have opened up the opportunity to achieve more perfect solutions for everyone. Personally, I see this as a mission I will carry throughout my career."

When asked about the skills, values or experiences he thought designers should have to change the world through their work, he cites empathy and the ability to create the optimal environment to facilitate change as fundamental — rather than trying too hard to create something new. He also stresses on the importance of practising one's craft, something that he personally keeps busy with in the studio everyday by juggling between design work, administrative tasks, meetings and workshops.

Looking forward, his vision for One Bite Design Studio's future is a clear and optimistic one. "We enjoy sharing space with others and believe that everyone should have equal rights in the public realm, so I hope to continue building alternative paths as a 'place maker' and urban curator. Ultimately, people are indispensable in the makings of a place, so we hope to bring more people together through our craft."

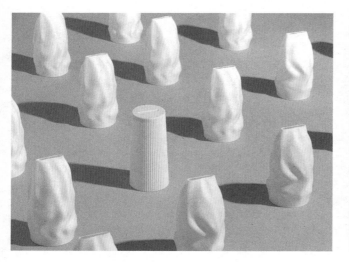

crafting plastics! studio

(2)

Pushing the Possibilities of
Materiality in Crafting the Future

It may come as no surprise, but the world is in the midst of a plastic crisis. With industrialisation and consumption levels reaching all-time highs over the last few years, plastic pollution has become one of the most pressing environmental issues affecting our planet, contributing to the acceleration of climate change. According to PlasticOceans.Org, over 380 million tons of plastic are produced each year — with up to 50% of that allocated to single-use purposes alone. The pandemic is further exacerbating the problem, as plastic debris from disposable face masks, medical equipment and takeaway boxes continue to multiply, especially in the Asian region (Source: Heinrich Böll Stiftung).

Now more than ever, it has become important for both individuals and organisations, regardless of specialty, to take a stand. Driven by passion and building on skill, design studios are starting to lead the pack in finding solutions to reduce the damage we are inflicting upon our surroundings to safeguard our future. crafting plastics! is one of the change makers to watch — an award-winning interdisciplinary design studio focusing on circular design and research in sustainability. The team is in the midst of developing a new generation of bioplastics by introducing innovative design concepts and prototypes, as well as bio-based solutions using 100% oil-free and compostable material.

Looking back on their journey so far, it is inspiring to note how curiosity led co-founders Vlasta Kubušová and Miroslav Král to come together for their cause as young design students, with the former graduating as a scenographer and costume designer; and the latter, a film producer. "We met at the Academy of Performing Arts in Bratislava when we were both studying there. Together, we worked on many theatre and film projects before shifting our focus onto material design. It was during this time that we began investigating alternatives for plastic materials, since there were very few options available in the market (even though the big material producers were claiming that they already had the solutions!). We understood then that every discipline was operating within its own bubble and found bridging the gap between science, creative production and consumer perceptions to be an excellent design task."

It was through Vlasta's collaborative design masters thesis at the University of Arts in Berlin with fashion designer Verena Michels called 'Crafting Plastics!' that they introduced the first prototypes of eyewear made from bioplastics as value-added products for the first time. Soon after, crafting plastics! studio was founded in 2016, with the aim to research, develop and use completely natural plastics for perishable but durable and beautiful products and intermediates. Although it is a relatively new studio, it has already picked up many accolades and exhibited around the world to date, underlined by a strong sense of purpose that continues to drive it forward — but keep the team grounded at the same time.

"...learning to respect and communicate/mediate between disciplines, as well as humans and non-humans, might be the most important skills we can learn."

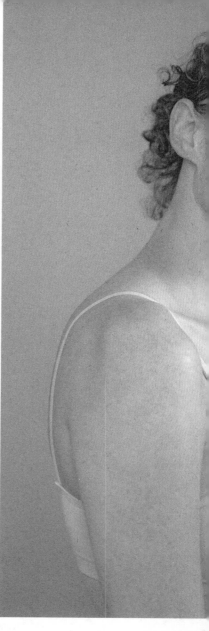

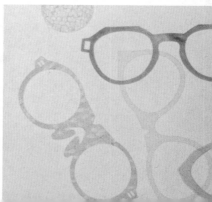

EYEWEAR COLLECTION 2: THESE WON'T OUTLIVE YOU!

crafting plastics!'s designer frames are made from a forward-thinking 100% bio-degradable mono-material. While the lifespan of the bioplastic eyewear range depends on the wearer, each pair of frames is strong and stable for as long as is needed. Once they're no longer serving their purpose, they can eventually be degraded in compost. What sets the frames apart is the team's innovative, uncompromising approach, resulting in sturdy and durable but malleable eyewear that can withstand temperatures of up to 110 degrees.

"At the forefront of our work is not just the environmental issues, but also our sociological points of view. The material culture that we as societies and communities have developed over the years cannot be changed immediately. Unfortunately, the feeling that most of us still have about plastic is that it should be durable, survive generations, etc. While some of us do go for biodegradable materials, the durable, resistant and synthetic materials often win at the point of purchase. When we first launched our eyewear made from our bioplastics blend, the question we often got was: 'Will it melt on my face when I am under the sun?' Of course the answer was obvious to us, but for most of the people who do not spend time reading about new materials, it was very normal to think so, and we think this is where designers can help out a lot — to create new materials and products, then bridge them with identities and narratives. Politics is also a crucial player in propagating the usage of a new material, in that it would be a very long process without new legislations. However, what ultimately excites and inspires us is the possibilities to create and enhance dialogues through our design solutions."

With their combined talent and experience, it would be easy for the duo to pursue new creative directions and challenge themselves in different fields rather than design for good — but Vlasta and Miro look towards the future with a crystal-clear vision, deftly handling all the challenges that come their way. "When it comes to designing for good, the question is really about what 'good' actually means and if we should be designing for something 'better' than the status quo instead. We believe that everything that comes out of the hands of a designer should already be designed for good, with the intention of producing positive outcomes. For us, it is about taking not just the final user into consideration but also everything around that is connected with it."

The duo are also no strangers to hate or doubt, which is a common issue faced by pioneers looking to start something new in pursuit of their passions or dreams. "There will be many naysayers who tell you that what you do is not good enough, not relevant, not important enough, and that you should follow a particular path because that is what will save the world. Many people or businesses who benefit from the traditional, linear economic system are still pushing green innovation away using vague arguments; mostly based on one point conveniently ripped from the overall context. The biggest challenge is to acknowledge that one single innovation won't make everything better and as hard it sometimes can be, there has to be constant mutual collaboration between everyone along the value chain. We also learned that the better we express our concepts and values at the beginning of collaboration, the smoother the process will be."

With a seemingly heavy burden on their shoulders, it would seem hard for studios like crafting plastics! to balance between pushing creative boundaries vs. commercial success. However, the team are united in their efforts. "We have never only had one focus in terms of creating limited artworks or products for commercial use. Therefore, when exploring materials, we want to push their limits to see where they can be used, where it makes the most sense, what the new properties or aesthetics can bring us — and so forth. We find the balance between science, design, our studio and research practice to achieve our goals. Sometimes, it is hard to put us in a box because we are perched the intersections of different disciplines and approaches, but this is what we love about it. Balancing helps us to stay flexible and find a way to sustain ourselves, which can be very hard in research-based design practices. We hope to create value, show what is possible with new materials, as well as navigate and help accelerate change in the acceptance of the new materials."

At the end of the day, they acknowledge that designing for good is crucial for growing as a designer — and a human being as a whole. "Sometimes, you have to learn completely new, unexpected skills that you were not taught in design school. Most of the time, you have to figure out the context to be sure about the consequences, and this requires respect towards others' opinions beyond your own ego. If we take designing for good as a general direction to create valuable projects for society and nature, then constantly learning to respect and communicate/mediate between disciplines, as well as humans and non-humans, might be one of the most important skills we can learn. While having enough power to sustain and make a living through a research-based, non-academic start-up is also a challenge, in the end, what else would we do if not design for good?"

CP!S FOR SCHLOSS HOLLENEGG FOR DESIGN, WALDEN EXHIBITION

The Arch represents the border between two worlds, where the polished meets the raw; tradition meets innovation; and the past meets the future. In this in-between space at Schloss Hollenegg, the crafting plastics! team decided to join poetic and technological forces to create an immersive but subtle and sustainable site-specific installation combining two natural materials: their NUATAN bio-plastic sheets, representing a new sustainable generation of plastic, and wood as the locally sourced, traditionally sustainable one. The project has since been expanded to include the creation of functional furniture pieces, including a bookshelf (Collection 9).

BIOPLASTIC DIFFUSORS (i–ii)

Scents are linked to our memories, while materials are linked to almost all human activities as well as the consequences that come along with their use. Through their bioplastics diffuser, the crafting plastics! team wanted to discover the relationship between the mystery of scents and the new innovative alternative to plastics to help people navigate between the natural and synthetic. The team 3D-printed analogue diffusors and two types of essences, created in collaboration with scientist Karol Červenčík.

NUATAN TO GO – BIOPLASTIC TABLEWARE & SAMPLE PACK (iii–iv)

Setting out to replace the traditional single-use cups in cafes, festivals and markets with a natural alternative that can decompose at the end of its lifecycle, NUATAN by crafting plastics! studio offers a closed-loop system as a bio-plastic alternative. One of the first products from their series is a reusable TO-GO coffee cup made of 100% renewable resources. Completely biodegradable, bio-compatible and able to withstand up to 100°C. the cup can last as long as needed for the typical consumer product and be easily disposed of into industrial compost. Since then, the team has developed a range of stylish tableware, as well as a sample pack of materials for potential partners who are into collaborations and innovations.

When talking about what is to come and what designers could do to pivot their work towards making a difference, the duo look to their daughter, the embodiment of the next generation, to guide them and cite diversity as a key value they are keen to pass on. They also believe that tenacity and working together with the like-minded will eventually lead to the transformation needed to turn the future around.

"Designers today have great opportunities to be the ones who can integrate many approaches and skills into comprehensive and constructive dialogues about what can be changed for the better. What we see as important is the courage and ability to keep holding on. They need to keep reminding themselves about why are they doing what they are doing, what their motivation is, as well as the skills they need to listen and connect. Our goal is to translate bio-based materials into practice and help to make a positive impact on different scales. We really hope to become an inspiration for the younger generation, for which there will be no other option than just design for good! On the other hand, we also hope to introduce solutions to industries to get closer to carbon neutrality. In the near future, we are going to focus more on collaborations with biologists to create bio-materials that minimise our burden on natural resources. We hope to continue new research on aroma-active bio-materials and living materials as part of our research, on top of introducing new bio-based solutions for the eyewear industry in the next year."

(iv)

WeTransfer

Championing Creativity
through Bytes of Humanity

[P. 274 Clockwise from Top Left]
Influence Podcast;
Enough Is Enough by Ashley
Lukashevsky;
WeTransfer Against Gun
Violence Wallpaper 2018

According to the 2021 World Development Report by WordBank.Org, global internet traffic was estimated to be more than 3 zettabytes — or 3,000,000,000,000 gigabytes — in 2020; which was roughly equivalent to 325 million households watching Netflix simultaneously. Without even having to put this ginormous number into context, it goes to show just how much we've come to rely on digital tools and services to go about our daily lives in this digital age. Coupled with the pandemic pushing us further towards online communication, this upward trend is unlikely to change.

Amid everything that has been happening over the last few years, WeTransfer has been quietly making its presence felt as a strong advocate of the creative community and its approach to humanising its platform to help those in need. What started out as a quick and simple file-sharing site has evolved into a force for positive change, deemed by Fast Company as one of the 10 most innovative social good companies in the industry. With close to 80 million monthly users in 187 countries and 2 billion files transferred monthly, its potential for making an impact continues to grow, especially for artists and illustrators looking to get their work out to the world.

Co-founder and Chief Creative Officer Damian Bradfield looks at the company's journey so far as a natural progression. "It's become much more of a trend nowadays to think about being a good business, and it's certainly being demanded much more from consumers of brands today, who are having to consciously put money where their mouth is. We've been doing it for ten years, really, because we had a gift. In the literal sense, we had a huge number of users who used the service really early on, giving us the amazing opportunity to be able to share the stories we create. Wee've known that it's su- per difficult for creatives to get exposure in popular media, even if they've been working hard for years, and we did our best to help a lot of illustrators like Jean Jullien, Malika Favre and Noma Bar earlier in their careers. While I'm not saying that we're responsible for their success, I'd like to think that we played some part in bringing their work to a wider audience. Personally, I believe in supporting the underdog. The upstart who needs to get a foot on the first rung of the ladder."

For several years now, WeTransfer has given away 30% of its ad space to support the arts and causes it believes in, as can be seen the moment you arrive on their often-colourful landing page, where you almost forget the function you were there to fulfil in the first place. While he has always felt privileged to be able to share great work and reach so many people, Damian is bittersweet about the current way with which the company chooses talents to showcase. "When it came to featuring someone's work or writing about them, it used to be a very casual, informal and organic process. Fortunately and unfortunately today, and I say this with best intent, we have a 12-person strong editorial team in London who plans everything up to three months in advance and often far longer. There is more structure to our planning because we have a very strong commitment to diversity. We try to ensure that we represent every gender and work across every single continent so that our content is balanced and timed well."

As author of 'The Trust Manifesto: What You Need to Do to Create a Better Internet', a documentation of his personal thoughts and experiences on the topic of transparency, as well as a trustee for Alexander McQueen's Sarabande foundation (sarabandefoundation.org) and Chair of the University of the Underground (universityoftheunderground.org), Damian wears many hats — and his heart on his sleeve. Among all the work he has been doing, his favourite initiative to date is WeTransfer's very own foundation, The Supporting Act (thesupportingact.org), which was set up to inspire, support and facilitate a new generation of creatives.

"We have created and supported so many projects over the years, but for me, they all really culminated into the big one this year. The Supporting Act is the formalisation of a lot of the organic work we have been doing over the years — from co-funding gallery exhibitions, museum events, and anything else that might be relevant for artists, to building partnerships and giving scholarships to institutions like Central Saint Martins. Through the act, 1% of our revenue will now go towards supporting creatives and start-ups because at the end of the day, money is still the most direct and useful resource for them. We've just appointed our Board of Trustees, which include Tala Madani, Beatrix Ruf, Peggy de Jonge and Gilles Peterson; and I'm about to spend the next six months with a team in Spain doing as much in-depth research as we can to work out which problems we can address and how best to allocate our time and money toward solving them. All our efforts will be completely transparent, as we try to shine a bit of a spotlight on the sector itself."

When it comes to the difficult business of balancing commercial objectives with altruistic ones like designing for good, Damian is clear about where WeTransfer stands and where it is headed. "We try and focus on being a good business first and foremost, and from that, work on good design. WeTransfer has millions of users all over the world, and when you have so much influence, you want to wield it well. Over the last century, we lost our understanding of why we exist and why companies exist. Shareholder value took hold and we no longer focused on the employee or customer, but on the individuals with the most to gain. By focusing on simply delivering products and services that are genuinely necessary and understand that as an employer we carry a huge weight in providing satisfaction and income for families all over the world, it's easy to have a shared mission — as it is for any one individual."

ENOUGH IS ENOUGH 2018

In solidarity with the March For Our Lives demonstrations in March 2018 to demand for the end of gun violence and mass shootings, WeTransfer launched a 48-hour story-telling campaign to shine a spotlight on the urgent need for gun reform. It dedicated 100% of its advertising space, which is purchased by brands like Apple and Google, to a full-page wallpaper and site takeover in support of common sense legislation and the need for change. The campaign promoted a series of creative projects on WePresent, its editorial platform, to give a voice to raw, genuine stories about the lasting impact of gun violence, and perspectives from survivors, veterans and activists.

[Clockwise from Top Left] Enough is Enough by Henning Wagenbreth, Brian Elstak, and Camila Rosa

Animation stills from 'Don't Go Changing: Net Neutrality!' by Chris McDonnell

NET NEUTRALITY 2018

In 2018, US law makers moved to end net neutrality, one of the founding pillars of the internet which is based on the idea that internet service providers should treat all content flowing through their cables and cell towers equally. As an independent file transfer and sharing service, WeTransfer sought to inspire action from its creator community by partnering with local outfit, the Community Broadband Project, to create a fixed wireless network consisting of a series of wireless routers and antennas that offer net-neutral access to customers without the need for them to go through a big, traditional ISP. It also released a video to help illuminate the potential effects of the legislation for public awareness.

"I think you just have to be honest about who you are and how you operate — because we've got so much more to learn."

"I'd like to think that we can be a beacon for others to follow. There is no doubt that society is better informed than ever before and there is no question that climate change is real. WeTransfer cannot solve it alone and I would like to think that we are helping to demonstrate an alternative approach to business that others will follow. We also hope to offer the consumer complete transparency around data usage and their carbon footprint, so we can begin a conversation around how to reduce the latter through using the Internet. As we grow as a Certified B Corporation, we have to reduce our carbon emissions by 30% and want to make sure that we're not just talking the talk — that's a real challenge."

The only global certification of its kind today that measures a company's entire social and environmental performance, WeTransfer's B Corporation Certification is well-deserved, but Damian acknowledges that there is so much more to be done.

"I don't know that you can really be promoting sustainability without fundamentally changing your business practices, and that's not something you can easily do. I think there are amazing examples where major institutions have really changed in direction, but they had to take some pretty painful decisions to do it. Consumers are so much wiser these days, with so much more information at their fingertips. There is a far greater understanding of how things work and are produced. I think you just have to be honest about who you are and how you operate — and be open and willing to learn. I think it's super important that we try to push away from plastics and fossil fuel to different forms of energy, but before moving the entire automobile to electric perhaps we need to slow down and assess the life expectancy and production cycle of electric vehicles? We need to consider a complete cradle to cradle approach to production. Is the Model S really going to last the next 50 years? I doubt it. And I think the most important learning anybody has shared so far, is that it's all about moderation. Our generation basically got distracted with the ability to use plastic and be able to consume and consume and consume, to increase shelf life and buy anything from anywhere. And that's the one thing that we've got to try and change — habits of consumption to moderation."

Illustration for 'We're going to need a smaller shoe' article by Daniel Liévano

While the future of WeTransfer will indeed be an exciting one to follow, Damian's upcoming personal projects are also not be missed, as he looks toward the release of his new dystopian internet graphic novel and plans to make a film on good business. Driven by his belief in the power of learning and creativity, the way with which he completes WeTransfer's tagline for us is testament to his capabilities as a visionary leader who will continue to steer the company forward with deft hands.

"Behind every great idea is an individual. I say this in a contrarian manner, because everybody today talks about collaboration and sharing ideas as being optimal, but I actually really believe that a great idea comes from yourself, often alone. There is so much fantastic work being produced today, but I think a lot of them could be so much better if they were a bit more opinionated and perhaps solitary. The great thing is, we now have everything we need to do it — there's just so much at your fingertips. COVID-19 may have accelerated the need for online collaboration tools and we obviously produce these ourselves, but collaboration is important only at the right moments. I am all in favour of collaboration once one has sat in solitude with an idea for a while, but too many a great idea, a gut-wrenching moment of genius, is destroyed in a group brainstorm. There will come a time when we're thoroughly bored of collaboration and longing for some sort of individualistic mindset or belief that's just a little bit more pointed, perhaps."

CARBON FOOTPRINT 2020

In 2020, WeTransfer became a Certified B Corporation, joining companies like Patagonia, Ben & Jerry's and The Guardian that balance people, planet and profit to use business as a force for good. As such, it has strengthened its commitment towards reducing carbon emissions, starting with carbon neutrality by the end of 2020 and a pledge to reduce emissions by 30% by 2025. On top of being honest and transparent in its efforts and collaborating with like-minded partners in its operations, it will be focusing on using renewable energy sources, making intelligent and sustainable purchases, as well as empowering its employees to achieve its goals as one.

BIOGRAPHY & CREDITS

BIOGRAPHY

&Walsh
PP 188-191, 198-201

&Walsh is a creative agency in NYC specialising in branding and advertising. The team believes in creating beautiful, emotion-driven work that functions for its clients' goals and resonates with their audiences.

Anjela Freyja
PP 202-205

Anjela Freyja is an independent creative director and designer working independently in New York and London. Her work is known for creative storytelling that combines multiple visual artistic mediums to communicate compelling stories, visual identities, and social activist platforms through 360° brand experiences encapsulating print, digital and environmental applications.

Ariadna Sala Nadal
PP 100-103

Ariadna Sala Nadal is a graphic and product designer from Barcelona who defines herself as a sensitive and dynamic person, always ready to reflect. She dedicates her time and energy to studying design to materialise her values, address her concerns, and find improvements to the problems that affect our society.

Citron Studio
PP 130-133

Citron is a brand design studio led by Jennifer James Wright. Founded upon the simple notion that design is best used for good, it collaborates with clients to bring forth positive change, whether by giving a visual voice to cannabis activists or creating coffee packaging with a smaller environmental footprint.

CoDesign Ltd
PP 050-069

Co-founded by Eddy Yu and Hung Lam in 2003, CoDesign Ltd specialises in providing holistic branding solutions. CoLAB, a collaborative platform for social innovation through design, was set up in 2011 to synergise the forces of commercial, cultural and social entities to consciously promote social betterment through creativity.

Cori Corinne
PP 090-095

Cori Corinne is an independent art director and designer based in Ohio. She combines her experience in design and background as an artist to solve problems, tell stories, and create compelling brand experiences, seeking to bring thoughtful, visual narrations into every aspect of design.

crafting plastics! studio
PP 266-273

crafting plastics! studio was founded in 2016 by product designer Vlasta Kubušová and production designer Miroslav Král. The studio is based between Berlin and Bratislava. Realising dynamic research and innovation in materials and design, it provides a base for interdisciplinary progress towards enjoyable sustainability and more transparent production.

democràcia estudio
PP 114-117

Founded in Valencia, democràcia is a collaborative project led by Javi Tortosa focusing on brand development projects through visual language. The team creates global brand experiences that balance images and words according to its graphic vision, underlined by a solid concept.

Familia
PP 174-177

Familia is a graphic design and communication studio in Barcelona with extensive experience in corporate identity, signage and editorial design. The team develops contemporary and aesthetic projects with a clear commitment to functionality, adding value, and meeting the particular needs of each client.

Fieldwork Facility
PP 108-113, 160-163

Fieldwork Facility is a design studio for uncharted territories that works in the intersection of communication, innovation and place. Its projects span campaigns, brands and experiences, as well as product and service innovation.

For The People
PP 070-088

For The People is a collective of designers, writers and strategists with the goal of creating work that creates social and economic impact.

G.F Smith
PP 142-145

G.F Smith are British makers and curators of the world's finest specialist paper since 1885. Offering expertise, knowledge and experience, they partner with the world's leading luxury brands, creative designers, and print specialists to provide inspired solutions for 21st century needs. Their vision is to demonstrate a love of paper and fascination for its limitless possibilities, and the power and beauty of the physical and tactile.

Goods
PP 146-149

A venture by Heydays Studio, Goods designs consumer brands, retail experiences and packaging for people and the planet. Based in Oslo, the studio works internationally with ambitious clients that challenge the categories they are in. It is also the creator of 'Index', an open source framework for sustainable packaging design.

Graphéine
PP 134-137

Founded in 2002 by like-minded, lively designers from various walks to life who are addicted to imagery, Graphéine is a graphic design and branding agency where all team members use their skills to complement the whole. It specialises in projects involving brand creation, visual identities, publishing, signages and web design.

IDEOLOGY DESIGN STUDIO
PP 206-209

Founded in 2018, IDEOLOGY is an award-winning multidisciplinary design studio based in Kota Kinabalu and Kuala Lumpur. Aiming to raise the bar in the design industry, the team pushes its limits in every project to deliver strategic and quality design, tailored to its clients' needs by building long-term relationships.

Seachange

Seachange is a full-service creative agency based in Auckland. The team strives to transcend categories, challenge perceptions and endure, combining multiple disciplines like branding, packaging, digital, art direction and book design for a diverse range of clients.

Sonder Collective

Sonder is an interdisciplinary design collective that creates processes for meaningful social change to be imagined and enacted. Through its projects and collaborative models, the team works towards a more equitable future.

SPACE10

SPACE10 is a research and design lab on a mission to create a better everyday life for people and the planet. At its core, the team prioritises a collaborative approach with an ever-growing network of forward-thinking specialists and creatives. SPACE10 is proudly supported by and entirely dedicated to IKEA.

Special Projects

Special Projects is an award-winning design and innovation agency based in London. It helps brave companies to discover new opportunities by revealing user needs and transforming them into tomorrow's most loved customer experiences and products.

Studio Dumbar

Studio Dumbar (part of Dept) is an international agency with Dutch heritage, specialising in visual branding and motion. Comprising talented individuals from all over the world, the team produces equally diverse, encompassing work for a variety of clients both large and small — from business and government to cultural and non-profit.

Studio Rejane Dal Bello

Studio Rejane Dal Bello creates work that is meaningful, engaging and lasting. The team gets to the heart of its projects to uncover what truly matters. Besides clearly communicating a brand's beliefs in a striking, moving and effective way, it collaborates with people who share the same passion for design.

Superunion

Superunion is a global brand agency built on a revolutionary spirit and the power of ideas to create positive, meaningful change. The team are experts in brand strategy, design, communications, and brand management, working across 17 countries for some of the world's most iconic brands alongside technology unicorns, ambitious start-ups and inspiring not-for-profits.

TEMPLO

TEMPLO is a branding and digital agency specialising in creativity for change. From helping to arrest war criminals and being a part of the controversial 2015 UN Gaza Conflict inquiry to producing groundbreaking work exposing Sri Lanka's sexual violence in conflict, its work has received global recognition and accolades.

WeTransfer

Beyond quick and simple file-sharing, WeTransfer has grown into a collection of tools designed for and inspired by the creative process. As it continues to evolve, creativity remains at the heart of everything it does – because while not every idea will change the world, every world-changing idea has to start somewhere.

CREDITS

Production:
Entropico

Photography:
James Dore

Derwent Valley Identity
For The People

Client:
Derwent Valley Council

Illustration:
Ilana Bodenstein

Balisa
Ariadna Sala Nadal

Special Credit:
Elisava School of Design
and Engineering

LINKAGE
Kosuke Takahashi

Concept / Product Design /
Project Lead:
Kosuke Takahashi

Communication Design:
Natsumi Wada

Interactive Design:
Momoka Nakayama

Art Direction / Graphic Design:
Kanako Ichimori

Haptic Design:
Hayato Tabata

A Better Source
Citron Studio

Photography:
Sarah Natsumi Moore

Research Assistance:
Alice May Du

Site Development:
Justin Levinsohn

Extract
G.F Smith

Exhibition:
MadeThought

Festival Simbiòtic
Pràctica & Guillem Casasus

Copy:
Dalmaus

Photography & Production:
Kiwi Bravo

Make Up:
Lara Güell

Styling:
Clara Borrull

Mody Road Garden
KaCaMa Design Lab

Photography:
supfilm

What's Your Proposition?
TEMPLO

Development:
Patrick Altair McDonald

Photography:
Taylor Harford,
Sarah Packer (Event)

Videography:
Round One Films

emograms with LOVE
kissmiklos

Photography:
Eszter Sarah (Gallery)

Special Credits:
Pi Studio, Lotte Gallery,
Lotte Department Store

Dr Giraffe Book Series
Studio Rejane Dal Bello

Words & Story:
Jayshree Viswanathan

Medical Strategy:
Stefan Liute

Alzheimer Nederland
Studio Dumbar

Photography:
Pieter Claessen (Brochures)

Relief Watch — Humanitarian Accountability, Reimagined
Sonder Collective

Special Credit:
The Humanitarian Policy Group
at The Overseas Development
Institute, Humanity United

Smart Distancing System
Jólan van der Wiel & Nick Verstand

Special Credit:
Singa

NIN_NIN
Kosuke Takahashi

Product Design:
Kosuke Takahashi

Robot Communication:
Ory Yoshifuji

Production:
Tomohiro Sawada

Planning:
Atsushi Otaki

Art Direction:
Kentaro Itonori

Design Engineering:
Yusuke Kamiyama

Fashion Direction:
Hatsuki Sugai

Art Design:
Takushi Okina

Design:
Masae Snow

Photography:
Michiko Kiseki

PLASTIC PAPER
PLACEHOLDER/Shō Shibuya

Copywriting:
Cole Kennedy

Design:
Chih Hsuan Hou

Series A — Forget Fashion
Public Positions

Project Partner:
Champions Without Borders e.V.

Development:
Maximilian Sprengholz

Photography:
Jan Kapitän

Series B — Poster Stories
Public Positions

Poster Design:
Florian Seidel

Photography:
Nora Heinisch

Series C — Positivisions
Public Positions

Special Credits:
Sebastian Bareis, Eric
Dannebaum, Dirk Gössler,
Jan Kapitän, Matthias Klinger,
Pascal Schönegg

Photography:
Sandra Gramm

An Object x Mobile Wardrobe Series
One Bite Design Studio

Collaboration:
Look Matters, Jupyeah

JUNK! Woodworking
One Bite Design Studio

Client:
Art Promotion Office, Leisure and

Cultural Services Department,
HKSAR Government

Collaboration:
Hong Kong Sculpture Society,
Coutou Woodworking Studio

Photography:
Tai Ngai Lung

PP. 258, 262-263

Design District Hong Kong
One Bite Design Studio

Client:
Tourist Commission &
Hong Kong Design Centre

Project Co-ordinator:
Dream of Tomorrow

Collaboration:
&dear, Arm Charm, Breakthrough
Art Studio, Creativity is, Delia
Indra Yoga, Foodyfree, Hong
Kong Architecture Centre,Hong
Kong Arts Centre, Hong Kong
Art School, Hong Kong Design
Institute, HKWALLS, iDiscover,
New Youth Barbershop, Nowhere
Boys, ohmykids, Oi Kwan Barbers,
PLOTZ, streetsignhk, The Bottle
Shop, SNL Beer, Viva Blue House,
Adonian Chan, Calvin Kwok,
Choi Kim Hung, Mak Kai Hang,
Renatus Wu, Yao Cheuk Ni, Loiix
Fung, Antonie LI, Maggie Wong,
Kiwi Chan

Photography:
Tai Ngai Lung

Videography:
Marvin Tam

PP. 262-263

Siu Hei Court Sportsground
One Bite Design Studio

Client:
Gaw Capital / People's Place

Collaboration:
W.f.b. Mantra Institute Nursery
School, The Lotus Association
of Hong Kong Siu Hei Court
Kindergarten, Yan Chai Hospital
Law Chan Chor Si Primary School,
Lung Kong World Federation
School Limited (LKWFS) Lau Tak
Yung Memorial Primary School,
New Life Psychiatric Rehabilitation
Association Institute

Typeface Design:
Never-Never

Photography & Videography:
Gaw Capital / People's Place,
Tai Ngai Lung, Marvin Tam

PP. 264-265

Project House
One Bite Design Studio

Photography:
Tai Ngai Lung, Enid Chan

PP. 264-265

Community Event at Kennedy Town
One Bite Design Studio

Client:
Little Creatures Brewing Hong Kong

Collaboration:
Caritas Mok Cheung Shui Kun
Community Centre, iDiscover

P. 266

Ulimited 3D-Printed Vases
crafting plastics! studio

Photography:
Adam Šakový

P. 266

Collection 6: Bioplastic Tableware
crafting plastics! studio

Photography:
Patricia Kvasnovska

P. 266

Breathe In / Breathe Out
crafting plastics! studio, OFFICE
MMK

Photography:
Adam Šakový

PP. 268-269

Eyewear Collection 2: These won't outlive you!
crafting plastics! studio

Photography:
Evelyn Bencicova

PP. 270-271

CP!S for Schloss Hollenegg for Design, Walden Exhibition
crafting plastics! studio

Photography:
Adam Šakový

PP. 272-273

Bioplastic Diffusors
crafting plastics! studio

Photography:
Adam Šakový

PP. 272-273

NUATAN TO GO — Bioplastic Tableware & Sample Pack
crafting plastics! studio

Photography:
Adam Šakový (iii),
Patricia Kvasnovska (iv)

PP. 274-277

Enough Is Enough 2018
WeTransfer

Illustration:
Ashley Lukashevsky (P. 274),
Henning Wagenbreth, Brian
Elstak, Camila Rosa (P. 276-277
Clockwise from Top Left)

Courtesy WePresent by
WeTransfer

PP. 278-279

Net Neutrality
WeTransfer

Animation "Don't Go Changing:
Net Neutrality!, 2018":
Chris McDonnell

Music:
Adam Roth, Allen Blickle

P. 280

Carbon Footprint
WeTransfer

Illustration for "We're going to
need a smaller shoe" article:
Daniel Liévano

Acknowledgement

We would like to thank all the designers and companies who were involved in the production of this book. This project would not have been accomplished without their significant contribution to its compilation. We would also like to express our gratitude to all the producers for their invaluable opinions and assistance throughout this entire project. Its successful completion owes a great deal to many professionals in the creative industry who have given us precious insights and comments. And to the many others whose names are not credited but have made specific input in this book, we thank you for your continuous support the whole time.

Future Editions

If you wish to participate in viction:ary's future projects and publications, please send your website or portfolio to submit@victionary.com